BOOK 2 Listen Up, Talk Back

James Bean and Yoshihito Kamakura

 SEIBIDO

Published and distributed by Seibido Publishing Co., Ltd.

Created and developed by
International Language Teaching Services Ltd
First floor, 1 Market Street
Saffron Walden, Essex CB10 1JB, UK

help@ilts.info
www.ilts.info

First published 2020
Copyright © International Language Teaching Services Ltd 2020

Editor: James Bean
Illustrations: Dani Geremia
Cover and text design: Clare Webber www.clarewebber.co.uk
Photographs: Shutterstock, Bigstock

ISBN 978-4-7919-7224-1

音声ファイルのダウンロード／ストリーミング

CD マーク表示がある箇所は、音声を弊社 HP より無料でダウンロード／ストリーミングすることができます。下記 URL の書籍詳細ページに音声ダウンロードアイコンがございますのでそちらから自習用音声としてご活用ください。

http://seibido.co.jp/ad597

Preface

Listen Up, Talk Back is a comprehensive listening and speaking course for elementary to intermediate students. This two-book series has been specially written for Japanese college and university students. The topics in *Listen Up, Talk Back* reflect the kinds of situations students come across both when studying in their home country and abroad. The topics are practical, useful, and generative. Students will be able to use the language they practice in *Listen Up, Talk Back* in everyday situations. Students are introduced to characters whom they will be able to relate to. This approach greatly helps them to tap into existing knowledge, experience, vocabulary, and structures, and to build upon this further.

Each unit focuses on a topic and related vocabulary, functions, and grammar. Students are also provided with a wide range of speaking and listening activities and exercises. These have been carefully written to provide an appropriate amount of support in order to make each task challenging yet achievable.

How to use this book

Warm-up

The warm up activities introduce the topic of the unit. A visual image is provided to help establish the context. Students are invited to draw on and discuss their own experience of the topic. Key vocabulary for the unit is presented to allow for maximum comprehension of the listening tasks.

Listening activities

Listening is a key aspect of this series. Each unit provides three separate listening tasks. Each listening task consists of two to three activities. The listening activities initially focus on general understanding, followed by listening for details. General understanding activities may be to identify who is speaking or to identify the general topic of a conversation. Listening for detail activities include listening for numbers, completing tables with key information, and underlining the correct word in a sentence. Each activity is carefully designed to involve minimal responses as far as possible in order to allow students to focus on listening more than writing.

A wide variety of exercise types is used to maximize student engagement. In addition, students are exposed to a variety of listening texts such as conversations, advertisements, voicemail messages, and announcements. It is advised that teachers allow students to listen to each text a number of times. Students will need repetition of the listening texts in order to focus on the different demands of each activity.

Tips for Communication

These useful, practical tips for everyday communication support the following speaking activities. The tips are drawn from the conversations in the listening exercises, so students get a good sense of the context they relate to. The tips focus on things such as answering the phone, using idioms, addressing people formally and informally, and strategies for keeping a conversation going.

Speaking activities

Speaking practice is an important feature of this series. Each unit offers three opportunities for students to speak within the given topic area. Pair work is a key activity.

In *Talk with a Partner*, students practice simple spoken interactions based on a "chunk" of language they have heard in the Listening texts.

In *Develop Your Speaking Skills*, students first read a scripted dialog aloud, and then introduce different elements to create their own conversation, communicating more freely within the language structures they have encountered. If appropriate, teachers could invite pairs to "perform" their conversations to the rest of the class.

Each of the above exercise types is accompanied by a language box that sets out key vocabulary, expression, and patterns.

In the third speaking activity of each unit, students practice in a range of communication channels, including voicemail messages, advertisements, and announcements. In some units, the third speaking activity gives students guidance to enable them to prepare and give a short talk or a more formal speech. Teachers should give students ample time and support as they prepare their talks or speeches. Encouragement and support is vital to making students feel comfortable about speaking in front of others.

Grammar Focus

In each unit, one element of grammar is highlighted and explained. The grammar point is drawn from the conversations in the listening exercises. A clear explanation is given with examples. The students complete exercises to consolidate their understanding of the grammar point.

はじめに

本書 Listen Up, Talk Back は初中級者向けリスニング・スピーキング力養成のためのテキストとして執筆されました。2つのシリーズ本から構成される本書は、特に日本人大学生を対象に構成されています。昨年 2020 年に刊行されたシリーズ 1 が英語学習初中級者に英会話の実践練習の導入を目指して作成されたのに対し、このシリーズ 2 は中級者を想定して作成されました。シリーズ 1 を終えた学習者が抵抗なく、継続してシリーズ 2 の学習に移行できるよう構成されています。

本書のトピックは日本人大学生が国内と国外で経験する英会話の場面を、実践的に、有用に、そして発展できるように設定しています。本書で学んだ表現はそのまま英会話で使用できます。教科書の登場人物は周りの人たちとの会話のやり取りを繰り広げます。この状況から学ぶことで、英会話で実際に使用される語句・表現・文構造・知識・経験などを疑似体験し、さらなるリスニング・スピーキング技能の向上を望むことができます。

本書の各課にて、1つのトピックについて関連する語句・機能・文法を取り上げます。様々なスピーキングとリスニングのタスクを用意し、能力を伸ばすため若干難しくはあるが、必ず回答可能な問題を豊富なヒントと指示とともに提供しています。本書ははじめに英語母語話者 Bean 氏が原稿を作成し、その内容を日本人英語教員である鎌倉が再構成しています。前書に引き続き、上記英語母語話者による英語教育の指導経験を基に、中級学習者が学ぶべき語彙や表現を提示しています。そして、鎌倉からの提案により「英会話文法」を充実させました。中高での英語学習ではあまり深く説明されないが、英語話者の視点や認知感覚を反映させた文法項目を日本人学習者が理解しやすいよう、例文とともに解説しています。

本書の出版の機会を頂いた成美堂社長佐野英一郎氏、と御協力を頂いた編集部の佐野泰孝氏、萩原美奈子氏、工藤隆志氏には大変お世話になりました。心からの感謝を申し上げます。

James Bean

鎌倉　義士

本書の使い方

Warm-up

各課冒頭にあるWarm-upでは、その課で学ぶトピックに関連する単語を確認します。教科書にある絵や画像から語を連想できるよう構成しています。学生の経験を引き出し、その後の会話練習につながるように関連する重要語句をここで学びます。

Listening

本書の中心となるリスニングは3つもしくは4つから構成されています。課前半のListening1と2では日本人学生タカシやヨーコが英語で会話するダイアログを聞き取り、その理解度を教科書内の設問で測ります。リスニングの内容は会話全体の理解から細部までの理解へと段階的に構成されています。話者は誰か、会話のトピックは何かなど全体的な理解から、数字の聞き取り、表の作成、正しい情報の選択など会話の詳細の理解までを本書で学習できます。リスニング内容を確認する設問は必要最小限の回答に抑え、学生がリスニングに集中できるよう配慮しています。学生が多種多様な英語による聞き取りを学ぶため、後半のListening3と4では一人の話者によるモノローグや広告、留守電メッセージ、告知のアナウンスなどを課題としています。英語による実生活で経験する音声を繰り返し聞くことで、学生の幅広いリスニング力を養います。

Tips for Communication

リスニングの会話内で使用されている英会話でのコツや秘訣を英語ネイティブ話者の視点から説明しています。その内容はフォーマルから親しげな会話の方法、会話を続けるコツ、電話での応対、イディオム・慣用句の使用まで多岐にわたります。英会話を潤滑に行うためのヒントを学生と共有してください。

Talk with a Partner

スピーキングは本書のもう一つの重要課題です。各課のトピックに関連する3つの会話練習を用意し、ペアワークを中心に展開します。chunkやset phraseと呼ばれる定形表現を使用しながら、学生が英会話を実践します。

Language Box

高頻度の定形語句や表現を使用することで、自然に会話が成立するよう構成してあります。

Develop Your Speaking Skills

Aパートにて学生は教科書のダイアログを読み、その会話を模倣することで会話の流れや、やり取りの方法を学びます。続くBパートにてLanguage Boxの表現を参考に取り入れ、学生が話したい内容をオリジナルの英会話として自由に表現できるよう段階的に練習します。

Speaking

課後半のListeningで聞いたモノローグを学生が練習します。会話以外の英語の表現方法を学ぶことで、多種多様な英語表現を聞き取り、発信する力を育むことを目的とします。

Grammar Focus

英会話に役立つ文法知識の確認をドリル練習の問題と共に提供しております。中学・高校で学んだ英文法の確認だけにならぬよう、英会話でどのように使用されているのかの点に注目し、例文とともに説明します。

CONTENTS

Here are the people you'll meet in the book.

He is 20 years old and he comes from Japan. Takashi is at university in the United States, and now he is living in a shared residence with other students.

Takashi

She is 20 years old and she comes from Virginia. Now Meg is attending university and is living in a shared residence with other students. But she lives close to her family.

Meg

She is 19 years old and she lives in Japan. Yoko is a university student.

Yoko

He is a 20-year-old student from California. Bill has moved to a different state to study at university. Now he's living in a shared residence with other students.

Bill

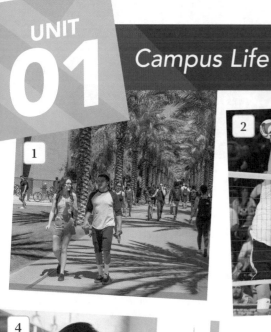

Warm-up

A Campus life is made up of many different activities. Look at what the people are saying. Match their words to the pictures. Write the numbers of the pictures.

> I don't really understand this paragraph. Can you help me?

> Good morning. I hope you've all done the reading I set you last week.

> Block it! Block it! Go, go! Yes!

> Hello! Are you interested in joining our club?

> Cellos, I'd like you to play louder. Let's try it again from the beginning.

> Are you headed to the library? I'm going that way, too. Do you mind if I walk with you?

B Work with a partner. What other activities are part of campus life? Make a list.

Listening 1

 1-02

A 🎧 Takashi is asking about joining the University Recreation Center. Which things are included in membership, and which things have an extra fee? Check the correct box.

	INCLUDED	EXTRA FEE
1. Use of the gym	☐	☐
2. Fitness classes	☐	☐
3. Use of the climbing wall	☐	☐
4. Use of the pool	☐	☐

B 🎧 Listen again. Circle **T** for true or **F** for false.

1. Undergraduate students can join the Recreation Center for free.   T / F
2. The Recreation Center is closed on Sundays.   T / F
3. There is a discount if you buy ten fitness classes together.   T / F
4. Takashi has done rock climbing before.   T / F
5. Takashi wants to use the swimming pool.   T / F

Tips for Communication

Include, included, including

Takashi says: *Are the fitness classes included?*
He is asking if the classes come as a part of Recreation Center membership or are something extra. To *include* means to have something as a part of a total. We often use this word when talking about prices and deals.

Does membership include use of the swimming pool?
Does our accommodation include breakfast?
The tour package includes all meals, but alcoholic drinks are not included.

We use *including* to introduce a list of examples of things in a group.

The Recreation Center offers many activities, including rock climbing and volleyball.

Listening 2

 1-03

A 🎧 Takashi is asking for directions on campus. Listen and circle the correct words.

1. Takashi wants to go to the **Business Studies** / **Theater Studies** Building.
2. Takashi says he wants to go **on the shuttle bus** / **on foot**.
3. At Founders Avenue, Takashi should turn **left** / **right**.
4. Takashi needs to walk **along** / **across** the river.

B 🎧 Listen again. Fill in the blanks.

1. It's _____ a walk.
2. The campus shuttle bus comes past here every _____ minutes.
3. I'm not in a _____, and it's a nice day!
4. I'm Erica, by the _____.

Talk with a Partner

👥 Practice talking with another student about joining a group or program on campus. Choose a group or program from the box below. Ask about joining and about extras.

LANGUAGE BOX	
Student A	**Student B**
I'm interested in becoming a member of the ... How do I join?	I just need you to fill out this form.
Does that include ...? Are / Is ... included?	Yes, that's included. / No, you have to pay extra for ...

Groups or programs	Recreation Center	choir	environment group	study group
Included	use of gym	use of rehearsal room	gloves	use of library
Extras	use of climbing wall	sheet music	T-shirt and hat	notes

Grammar Focus

Gerunds after adjectives and prepositions

Takashi says: *I'm interested in becoming a member of the Recreation Center.*
When a verb comes after a preposition (for example *in, of, about, for*), the verb
takes the gerund form (*-ing*). This structure is often used after adjectives that
describe feelings. Here are more examples:

*Sam is **afraid of** flying.   I'm **sorry for** forgetting your name earlier.*
*I'm **nervous about** giving the presentation.   Joe is **keen on** hiking.*

Complete the sentences using the prepositions and verbs given in the gerund form.

1. Susan is excited _____ her new job. (**about** / **start**)
2. Max is proud _____ the singing contest. (**of** / **win**)
3. Let's go! I'm worried _____ the train. (**about** / **miss**)
4. John is fond _____ up words in the dictionary. (**of** / **look**)
5. I'm sick _____ at this place. Can we try somewhere new?
   (**of** / **eat**)

Develop Your Speaking Skills

A 👥 **Work in pairs and practice the dialog.**

A : Hi there. Can I help you?
B : Yes, I'm interested in becoming a member of the basketball club. How do I join?
A : Welcome to the basketball club. I'm excited about having you as a member.
B : Thank you. But I've never played basketball before. I'm worried about causing
   problems for others.
A : Not at all. Our coach is good at training beginners. You'll soon be a better player.

B 👥 **Now practice the dialog with different groups or clubs. Try to use gerunds
after adjectives and prepositions by choosing expressions from the box.**

LANGUAGE BOX	
B	**A**
I'm interested in becoming a member of the... club.	Welcome to the.... I'm ... .
Thank you. But I've never ... . before. I'm... .	Not at all. Our coach is ... .

Useful Words and Phrases
soccer, swimming, photography, dance, be keen on, be fascinated by, be pleased at, be thrilled at, be nervous about, be afraid of, be sorry for, injury, catch up, be experienced in

Listening 3

 1-04

A 🎧 Listen to the online video and fill in the blanks.

Welcome to **Midlands College**. This video is designed to **introduce** you to the **Student Counseling** and **Wellbeing** Service. Campus life can be **enjoyable**, but it can also be ¹_____. At the **Counseling** and **Wellbeing** Service, we **understand** that a **range** of issues can make it **hard** to **get** the **most** out of your time here at **Midlands**. **We're** here to **help**, with both **academic** and ²_____ counseling. Our **StudyWise** program offers **academic** counseling and **support** through a **range** of workshops to help you **improve** your **study**, **time-management**, and ³_____ skills. Our **personal** counseling service is **here** to **help** with issues like **managing stress** and **taking care** of your **mental** ⁴_____. It's simple to arrange a **confidential one-on-one** meeting with one of our **highly** qualified **counselors** and **psychologists**. If you **need** someone to ⁵_____ to, we're here. Why not **visit** the **Student Counseling** and **Wellbeing** Service and **find** out **more about** us? We're on **Level 1** of the **Lacey** Building, and we're ⁶_____ from **nine** to **five**, **Monday** through **Friday**.

B 🎧 Listen again. Circle T for true or F for false.

1. The StudyWise program offers counseling on personal issues.   T / F
2. The personal counseling service can arrange for students to meet with a psychologist.   T / F
3. The Student Counseling and Wellbeing Service is closed on weekends.   T / F

Read the Script Aloud

Now pretend that you are the narrator of the video. Read the script aloud. Include the words that you wrote to fill the blanks. Speak slowly and clearly. Use intonation—stress the important words (make them stronger). Practice by stressing the **bold** words in the script above. You may practice silently to yourself first. Then read the script aloud to a partner or to your class.

Warm-up

A What's wrong? Look at the pictures of people with different health problems. Match the problems to the pictures. Write the numbers of the pictures.

a cold _____   eye fatigue _____

a bad cut _____   a broken leg _____

a sore back _____   an upset stomach _____

B 👥 Now look at what these people say about their problems. Who is speaking? Discuss your ideas with a partner.

“Maybe it's something I ate.”

“I lifted something too heavy yesterday.”

“My nose is blocked and my throat is sore.”

“I won't be able to walk for another four weeks.”

“I've been staring at the computer screen all day.”

“I should have been more careful with that knife!”

Listening 1

 1-05

A  Listen to Meg calling the health clinic. Circle T for true or F for false.

1. This will be Meg's first visit to Green Street Health Clinic.   T / F
2. Dr. Tran works at Green Street Health Clinic on Wednesdays.   T / F
3. Meg will see a doctor today.   T / F
4. Meg will see Dr. Tran.   T / F
5. Meg has class on Wednesday afternoon.   T / F

B Listen again. Circle the correct words.

1. I'd like to **make** / **have** an appointment to see Dr. Tran.
2. Now, when would you like to **come** / **be** in?
3. Is there anything **later** / **after** 3:30?
4. I'll put you **down** / **over** for 4:15 with Dr. Sanders.

Tips for Communication

Talking about times
When making appointments, we often need to talk about times. *Dr. Sanders has an appointment available at 2:30 this afternoon. Is there anything after 3:30? How about 4:15?* We can give times by saying the hour and the number of minutes after the hour. *two thirty   four fifteen*

But we can use other expressions, as shown in this table.

Time in numbers	Hour + minutes	Other expressions
6:00 a.m.	six (a.m.)	six o'clock (in the morning)
7:15 a.m.	seven fifteen	a quarter past seven
8:20 a.m.	eight twenty	twenty past eight
9:30 a.m.	nine thirty	half past nine
10:40 a.m.	ten forty	twenty to eleven
11:45 a.m.	eleven forty-five	a quarter to twelve
12:00 p.m.	twelve noon	twelve o'clock / midday
12:00 a.m.	twelve midnight	twelve o'clock at night

a.m. = before midday (morning); p.m. = after midday (afternoon/evening)
*Our flight departs at **seven thirty** tomorrow morning.*
*We should be at the airport at **six**.*
*Tonight's concert starts at **half past seven** and finishes at **nine o'clock**.*

Listening 2

🎧 1-06

A 🎧 Listen to Meg speaking with the doctor. Answer the questions.

  1. Where is Meg feeling pain?

    a. her heart **b.** her arm **c.** her forehead

  2. What does the doctor think may be causing the pain?

    a. working on the computer **b.** lifting heavy objects **c.** eating too much

B 🎧 Listen again. Fill in the blanks.

  1. The pain has been especially bad in the past three _____.

  2. It hurts when the doctor presses on Meg's elbow and her _____.

  3. Recently Meg has been doing a lot of _____.

  4. The doctor tells Meg it's important to take regular _____.

  5. After Meg finishes the work she's doing, she will take a two-week _____.

Talk with a Partner

👥 You are going to practice starting a conversation with a doctor. Choose one of the problems from the right-hand column of the box.

LANGUAGE BOX		
Doctor	**Patient**	
Good morning. What's brought you here today? / What can I help you with today?	Hello, Doctor. My ... is sore.	back stomach neck left foot right arm
And how long have you been having this pain?	Since the weekend For two weeks For the past two days It started a few days ago.	

Grammar Focus

Could for present and future possibilities

At the clinic, the receptionist tells Meg that her doctor is not there today and says: *I could see if he has an appointment time free tomorrow. Or you could see one of the other doctors here today.* We use *could* to talk about things that are possible in the future. This is a different use of *could* from when it forms the past tense of *can* (*I couldn't sleep last night*). Here is another example:

Don't swim today. The water is rough, and you could easily get into trouble.

We also use *could* to talk about things that are possibly true in the present and less possibly than *can*.

My phone is ringing. It could be my mother.

What time period does *could* refer to? Write past, present, or future.

1. I can't find William, but I guess he could be upstairs. _____
2. I could hear a noise outside, so I went to see what it was. _____
3. A package has been delivered. It could be the book I ordered. _____
4. Those clouds are getting closer. We could get caught in the rain! _____

Develop Your Speaking Skills

A Practice making an appointment. Work in pairs and practice the dialog.

Receptionist: Green Street Health Clinic. How may I help you?
Patient: Hello. I'd like to make an appointment to see Dr. Allen.
Receptionist: When would you like to come in?
Patient: Tomorrow afternoon, if possible.
Receptionist: Dr. Allen has an appointment available at 2:45 tomorrow. Could you come in then?
Patient: No, I'll be at work until 4 o'clock tomorrow.
Receptionist: Okay. Let me see. How about 4:45?
Patient: Yes, I could come in at 4:45.
Receptionist: All right, I'll put you down for 4:45 with Dr. Allen.

B Now look at Dr. Allen's schedule for Tuesday afternoon. The appointment times in blue are already taken. He only has four times available. Take turns being the patient calling in to make an appointment. Use expressions from the dialog above.

2:00	2:15	2:30	2:45	3:00	3:15	3:30	3:45	4:00	4:15	4:30	4:45

Patient 1: You are in class until 3:30.	Patient 2: You finish work at 4:30.
Patient 3: You start work at 3:00.	Patient 4: Your classes finish at 2:30 but then you start work at 4:30.

Listening 3

 1-07

🎧 Listen to the phone conversation. Circle the correct words.

1. Meg calls the doctor because her arm **still feels sore** / **feels worse**.
2. Meg **is still working on** / **has finished** her term paper.
3. Meg **has** / **has not** been doing the exercises the doctor gave her.
4. Meg **has** / **has not** been using her cell phone a lot.
5. The doctor says he might send Meg to have **an X-ray** / **an operation**.

Listening 4: *Voicemail*

 1-08

A 🎧 Listen to the message. Circle the correct answer. Why is Meg calling the clinic?

a. because she doesn't need to see the doctor any more
b. because she wants to make an appointment
c. because she needs to change her appointment time

B 🎧 Listen again and circle the correct answers.

1. What time does the clinic close on Fridays?
   a. 12 noon   b. 3 p.m.   c. 5 p.m.
2. When does Meg want to see the doctor?
   a. at 11:30 a.m.   b. before 3 p.m.   c. after 3 p.m.

Speaking: *Leave a Voicemail Message*

👥 Work with a partner. Take turns to practice leaving a voicemail message about changing your appointment. Use expressions from the box. Use different times and names.

LANGUAGE BOX

Hello, my name is ...
I have an appointment at ... this morning with Dr. ...
Unfortunately, I have to work / there's been a change to my schedule ...
... and I can't get to the clinic this morning.
I'm wondering if there's anything available later in the day, after ...
If someone could call me back and let me know, that would be great.
My number is ...
Once again, it's ... I can't make it to my appointment with Dr. ... at ...
Hoping to come in ... Thanks!

Doctors:

Dr. Benson	Dr. Kosky	Dr. Lim	Dr. O'Brien

My Favorite Things

Warm-up

A 👥 Do you have favorite things and favorite people? Talk with a partner. Answer the questions yourself and record your partner's answers.

	You	Partner
What's your favorite ...		
... pastime?	_____	_____
... subject?	_____	_____
... dish?	_____	_____
... color?	_____	_____
Who's your favorite ...		
... singer or musician?	_____	_____
... actor?	_____	_____
... athlete?	_____	_____
... writer?	_____	_____

B Here are the answers that one person gave to the questions above. Match the answers to the questions.

kaisen yakisoba   Naomi Osaka   JK Rowling   English   Ariana Grande
Leonardo DiCaprio   reading   yellow

Listening 1

 1-09

A 🎧 Listen to Yoko and her friend Dave talking about their favorite things. Look at the lists of things and write **Y** beside Yoko's favorites and **D** beside Dave's favorites.

Things to drink	Colors	Times of year	Sports to watch
Ice bubble tea ___	Maroon ___	Summer ___	Tennis ___
Apple juice ___	Scarlet ___	Spring ___	Gymnastics ___
Beer ___	Purple ___	New Year ___	Cycling ___
Cappuccino ___	Navy blue ___	Christmas ___	Baseball ___

B 🎧 Listen again. Circle the correct words.

1. What's **your** / **yours**?
2. I don't really have a **favorite** / **best** color.
3. I **really** / **don't** mind hot weather.
4. **My one** / **For me** it's Christmas time.
5. I love it **as** / **when** the Christmas decorations go up everywhere.

Tips for Communication

I don't mind

When Dave is talking about summer, he says: *I don't mind hot weather.*

This means he doesn't dislike it; it's okay for him.

When we use *mind* in this way, it means to dislike something, or feel unhappy or annoyed about it. But generally we only use it:

- in negative sentences with *don't* or *doesn't*:
  I don't mind a little rain.
  I don't mind living beside the airport.

- in questions:
  Q : *Do you mind if I sit here?*
  A : *No, go ahead.*
  Q : *Does anybody mind if Tina joins us this evening?*
  A : *No, she's welcome.*

We can also use *I don't mind* to say we don't have a strong preference for something.

Q : *Would you like orange juice or apple juice?*
A : *I don't mind. Either will be fine.*

Listening 2

 1-10

A 🎧 Listen to Yoko and her friend Marty talking about food. Circle **T** for true or **F** for false.

1. There's one dish that Yoko likes best of all.   T / F
2. Yoko likes pasta.   T / F
3. Marty knows how to make spaghetti carbonara.   T / F
4. Marty thinks barbecue ribs are fun to eat.   T / F

B 🎧 Listen again. Fill in the blanks.

1. I don't really have one favorite _____.
2. If we're talking about _____ dishes, I like any pasta dish.
3. It's so creamy and _____!
4. They're so tasty and good to eat, with that sticky _____.

Talk with a Partner

👥 Practice asking and talking about favorite things. Choose things from the box below or think up your own ideas. Ask and answer.

zoo animal   kind of pet   TV show   type of music   song   time of day
holiday destination   ice cream flavor   movie   fast food   sports team
tree   store   teacher   TV personality   politician

LANGUAGE BOX	
A	**B**
What's your favorite ...? Who's your favorite ...?	My favorite ... is ... I love ... / I really like ... Maybe ... For me it's ...
Really? Why? Yes, that's ...	Because ...

Grammar Focus

Tag questions

Yoko says to Marty: *You love barbecue ribs, don't you?*

The two words *don't you?* are a tag question. We use these when we think that what we are saying is correct and think the other person will confirm it.

Look at the patterns for tag questions:

Main verb in sentence	Tag	Example	"Yes" answer
Simple present	*don't* + pronoun	*You like sushi, **don't you?***	*Yes, I do.*
	doesn't + pronoun	*He sings well, **doesn't he?***	*Yes, he does.*
Simple past	*didn't* + pronoun	*We had fun, **didn't we?***	*Yes, we did.*

Note that the above patterns are for sentences where the main verb is not *to be*. For sentences with *to be*, the tag also has that verb: *This is a great song, **isn't it?***

A **Complete the tag questions with don't, doesn't, or didn't.**

1. You like chocolate, ＿＿＿＿＿ you?
2. Rob goes to art school, ＿＿＿＿＿ he?
3. These cookies taste great, ＿＿＿＿＿ they?
4. Marie went to Australia, ＿＿＿＿＿ she?

B **Write the tag questions.**

1. You know how to bake a cake, ＿＿＿＿＿?
2. John plays baseball every weekend, ＿＿＿＿＿?
3. Mr. and Mrs. Sato live in that building, ＿＿＿＿＿?

Develop Your Speaking Skills

A 👥 **Work in pairs and practice the dialog.**

A: Do you have a favorite food?
B: Definitely. Sushi.
A: Oh, yes! You love sushi, don't you?
B: Yes, I do. It's so tasty and good to eat with wasabi. You like it, too, don't you?
A: No, I don't. I don't like the smell of raw fish.

B 👥 **Now work with the same partner as you worked with for "Talk with a Partner." You have learned about their favorite things. Ask them about those things using tag questions. Use expressions from the box.**

LANGUAGE BOX	
A	**B**
Do you have a favorite...? Oh, yes! You love..., don't you? Yes, I do./ No, I don't. I don't like... because...	Definitely. .... Yes, I do. It's.... You like it, too, don't you?

15

Listening 3: *Short Talk*

 1-11

A 🎧 You are going to give a short talk about your favorite place. First, listen to the model talk below and fill in the blanks.

I'm going to tell you about my favorite place. It's where my family ¹_____ to go on vacation. It's a small ²_____ in the mountains, not far from my hometown. We used to load our car full of things and drive up and ³_____ in a house in the village for a week. The house is beside a stream. My brother and I used to love walking along a path beside the stream. What do I like about that place? It's a very peaceful, ⁴_____ place, with a nice view of the mountains. The people there are nice. I have lots of happy ⁵_____ of that place. Actually, I went back there last year, and it was just as I remembered it.

B Now think about a place you love. It may be a place from your childhood, or a place that's in your life now. Write your own short talk in the box below.
You may use the words or phrases in the language box to help you. Then present your short talk in class.

YOUR TALK

LANGUAGE BOX

I'm going to tell you about my favorite place.
It's where I / my family ... used to ...
It's a ...
I love / I used to love ...
What do I like about that place?
It's ...
The people there are ...
I have lots of happy memories of that place.

International Travel

Warm-up

A Match the words and phrases to the pictures. Write the numbers of the pictures.

taking off _____   checking in _____

landing _____   boarding _____

passport control _____   baggage collection _____

B 👥 Now look at what these people are saying. Which of the situations above are the people in? Discuss your ideas with a partner.

> ❝ Welcome aboard. Seat 19B is to the right. ❞

> ❝ Good morning. How many bags are you checking in today? ❞

> ❝ Please fasten your seatbelts for takeoff. ❞

> ❝ Oh, there's my suitcase! It's the blue one. ❞

> ❝ What is the purpose of your visit? ❞

> ❝ Ladies and gentlemen, welcome to Sydney, where the time is three minutes past eight. ❞

Listening 1

 1-12

A 🎧 **Listen to Bill talking with Tanya on the phone. Circle T for true or F for false.**

1. Bill needs to start packing for his trip.   T / F
2. Bill will be on two different flights tomorrow.   T / F
3. Bill will spend time in Los Angeles airport tomorrow.   T / F
4. Tanya will drive Bill to the airport tomorrow.   T / F
5. Bill is going to Australia for a vacation.   T / F

B 🎧 **Listen again. Circle the correct words.**

1. It **starts** / **departs** at 8:45.
2. Then I have a two-hour **layover** / **stay** in L.A.
3. It's 15 hours **one**-**stop** / **non**-**stop**.
4. How are you **getting** / **taking** to the airport tomorrow?

Tips for Communication

Wishing people a good trip

Tanya says to Bill: *Have a great vacation in Australia.*
She is expressing good wishes to Bill for his vacation. Bill answers: *Thanks, Tanya.*
When people are going away, it's nice to express good wishes to them. Here are more examples:

Have a wonderful time. I hope you have a nice time.
All the best for your trip. Enjoy your trip.
Good luck! Have a great time.

Note that some of these expressions are imperatives (*Have ...*, *Enjoy ...*). Often imperatives are used for more serious things like warnings (*Be careful!*) or instructions (*Stop here, thank you driver.*). However, they can also be used to express pleasant things (*Enjoy your meal. Have a nice day.*). The sense of this is similar to *I want you to enjoy ...* or *I want you to have ...*

Listening 2

 1-13

🎧 Listen to Bill talking with the check-in clerk at the airport. Choose the best answer for each question.

1. What is Bill's final destination?

(A) Los Angeles

(B) New York

(C) Sydney

(D) Melbourne

2. How many documents does the clerk ask to see?

(A) one

(B) two

(C) three

(D) four

3. What does the clerk want to do with Bill's bag?

(A) open it

(B) close it

(C) weigh it

(D) move it

4. What is Bill's seat number for the flight to Sydney?

(A) 5G

(B) A15

(C) 16A

(D) 36J

Talk with a Partner

👥 Practice talking with a friend about a trip. Choose a destination from the box below. Ask and answer, and express good wishes.

LANGUAGE BOX	
A	**B**
Hi, it's ... here. Are you all set for your big trip to ...? What time is your flight tomorrow? How are you getting to the airport? Well, have a great vacation in ... / Have a wonderful time in ... / I hope you have a nice time. / All the best for your trip. / Enjoy your trip.	Yes, I am. I just finished packing. It departs at ... I've bookcd a taxi. / I'll take the train. Thanks.

Vacation destinations

Hawaii	Bali	Vietnam	London	Fiji	Mexico

Grammar Focus

Simple present tense for future events

On the phone, Tanya asks Bill: *What time is your flight tomorrow?* Bill answers: *It departs at 8:45.*

At the check-in desk, the clerk says: *Your flight leaves from Gate 5. Boarding commences at 8:15.*

We can use the simple present tense for future events that are part of a schedule. Here are more examples, with verbs commonly used in this way:

*The train **arrives** at 2:15 p.m.   The concert **starts** at 7:30.*

*What time does the play **end**?*

*When do the stores at the mall **open**?*

*The supermarket **closes** at 9 p.m.*

Note that Tanya uses the present continuous when she asks: *How are you getting to the airport tomorrow?* We can use the present continuous to talk about plans we have made for the near future.

I'm taking *the train to the airport tomorrow.*

Complete each sentence with a verb from the box. Change the form of the verbs.

arrive	depart	open	close	end

1. My flight _____ at 6:30 this evening so I want to be at the airport by four.
2. Jenny's train _____ at 10:15 and she'll go straight to the hotel from the station.
3. The swimming pool _____ at five o'clock so we just have time for a quick swim.
4. The movie _____ at 11 o'clock. That's too late for me. Can we go to a shorter movie?
5. The ticket office _____ at nine o'clock this morning, but people started lining up to buy tickets at six!

Develop Your Speaking Skills

A 😊😊 **Practice talking about flights. Work in pairs and practice the dialog.**

A : What time does our flight leave?
B : At 3:15.
A : And which gate does it leave from?
B : It leaves from Gate 7.
A : And what time does boarding commence?
B : Let me see. Boarding commences at 2:45.
A : Good. Then we have time for a coffee!

B 🙇 Now look these flights and times. Choose different flights and have conversations like the example.

DEPARTURES					
Flight	Destination	Departs	Gate	Boarding	Remarks
AF75	MELBOURNE	9:20	5	8:45	ON TIME
SP51	SINGAPORE	9:45	9	9:15	ON TIME
HF294	HONOLULU	10:00	14	9:30	DELAYED
PF37	MANILA	10:10	6	9:40	ON TIME

Listening 3: *Airport Announcement*

 1-14

A 🎧 Listen to the airport announcement and fill in the blanks.

Good **morning**. This is the **pre**-**boarding** announcement for flight **TA476** to **Auckland**. At this **time** we invite **passengers** traveling with **small children** and those requiring special [1]_____ to **begin** boarding. **Please** come forward, and have your **boarding pass** and [2]_____ **ready** to **show** to our **staff**. **Regular** boarding will **commence** as **soon** as **pre**-**boarding** has been [3]_____. **First** and **business** class passengers will board **first**, followed by **economy** class passengers. **Economy** boarding will be by **row** number, **starting** with **passengers** in rows **63** to [4]_____. Your **seat** number can be **found** in the **bottom right hand corner** of your **boarding pass**. **Please** stay **seated** until your **row** is **called**. We remind **all** passengers that you are allowed **one** [5]_____ bag. Once **again**, at this time we are **pre**-**boarding** passengers with **small children** and those requiring **special assistance**. Thank you for your [6]_____. We wish you a **pleasant flight**.

B 🎧 Listen again. Circle T for true or F for false.

1. All passengers can get on the plane now. T / F
2. Passengers must show their boarding pass and passport. T / F
3. Passengers can bring two pieces of luggage on board. T / F
4. A passenger with a baby should board the plane now. T / F

Read the Announcement Aloud

Now pretend that you are making the announcement at the airport. Read the announcement aloud. Include the words that you wrote to fill the blanks. Speak slowly and clearly. Use intonation—stress the important words (make them stronger). Practice by stressing the **bold** words in the announcement above. You may practice silently to yourself first. Then read the announcement aloud to a partner or to your class.

Weather

Warm-up

A The weather often makes news. News stories begin with a headline giving the main idea of the story. Read the headlines and match them to the pictures. Write the numbers of the pictures.

a. ___

THOUSANDS FLOCK TO BEACHES ON HOTTEST DAY OF YEAR

b. ___

HEAVY SNOW BRINGS ICY ROADS AND SCHOOL CLOSINGS

c. ___

FLOODS CAUSE ROADS TO CLOSE

d. ___

BIG CROWD AT FOOTBALL FINAL DESPITE HEAVY RAIN

e. ___

FARMERS STRUGGLE AS DROUGHT CONTINUES

f. ___

Wild winds cause damage across city

B 👥 Work with a partner. Talk about a time when you have experienced one of the types of weather shown in the pictures.

Listening 1

 1-15

A 🎧 Listen to Yoko talking with her friend Marty on the phone. Circle the correct answer.

1. What is the purpose of Marty's call?
   a. to check whether the concert is still on
   b. to check whether Yoko wants to go to the park
   c. to tell Yoko that the concert has been canceled

2. Why does Marty think it might rain?
   a. He can see clouds in the sky.
   b. He checked the weather forecast.
   c. He heard the concert was being canceled.

3. What will they do if the concert is canceled?
   a. go home   b. stay in the park   c. go for a coffee

B 🎧 Listen again. **Answer Yes or No**.

1. Does Yoko want to go to the concert in the park? _____
2. Is the sky clear? _____
3. Does the weather forecast say it will definitely rain? _____
4. Do Yoko and Marty decide to go to the park? _____

Tips for Communication

I see what you mean
When Marty asks Yoko to take a look at the rain clouds, she says *I see what you mean*. This is a way of telling Marty that she understands what he is saying—there are rain clouds in the sky, so it could rain.   We can say *I see what you mean* even if we don't agree with what another person is saying. It's just a way of saying that you understand their point.
Keep an eye on
Marty says: *Let's keep an eye on the weather.*   To *keep an eye on* something means to watch and check it.   *Can you please keep an eye on the baby while I go to the bathroom?*   *When you're cooking something on the stove, keep an eye on it.*

Listening 2

A 🎧 **Listen to Yoko and her friend Dave. Circle T for true or F for false**

1. They are talking about tomorrow's weather forecast.   T / F
2. Yoko traveled by train this morning.   T / F
3. The electricity went out at Dave's place.   T / F
4. Yoko heard that the weather will clear by late morning.   T / F
5. They are in the library.   T / F

B 🎧 **Listen again. Fill in the blanks.**

1. Wow! We're having _____ weather today!
2. My umbrella was turned _____ as I was crossing the street!
3. I got here an hour _____!
4. If it keeps raining, the streets are going to be _____.
5. So, getting home could be _____.

Talk with a Partner

👥 Person A chooses an outdoor event and call person B. Person B chooses a weather forecast.

LANGUAGE BOX			
A	**Outdoor events**	**B**	**Weather forecasts**
Do you still want to go to the ...? Do you think it's going to rain? Do you think we should go?	concert in the park baseball game fair outdoor markets	Let me check the weather forecast. It says ... Yes, I ... / No, I ...	possible showers thunderstorms mainly fine dry and windy warm and sunny morning showers, clearing in the afternoon

Grammar Focus

Let me with infinitives

When Yoko goes to see what the weather is like outside, she says: *Let me look.* Later, she says: *Let me check the weather forecast.* Here the verb *let* is an example of the imperative. We use the imperative for commands, instructions, requests, or invitations (Give *me that. Turn right. Please close the door. Take a seat.*). In this case it is a request, but Yoko isn't really asking for permission to look out of her window. She's really saying: *Wait for a moment while I look.* We often use the structure *let me* + infinitive (without *to*) to introduce a request, offer, or proposal. Here are more examples:

That's a lot of boxes to carry. **Let me** *help you.*
I'm not sure if I'm free this weekend. **Let me** *see. Yes, I'm free on Sunday.*
Let me *know what I can bring to your party.*

Complete each sentence with *Let me* and a verb from the box.

guess	tell	ask	get	know

1. _____ you a question. Do you think this color suits me?
2. _____ you something. You need to start working harder.
3. What's for lunch? No, _____. Are we having noodles?
4. Oh, you spilled your coffee. Stay there. _____ you a napkin.
5. _____ what time you think you'll arrive.

Develop Your Speaking Skills

👥 Work in pairs and practice using Let me know.

A **Practice the dialog.**

A : Would you like me to bring anything to your party?
B : I'm not sure yet.
A : Well, let me know.
B : Thanks, I will.

B **Now ask and answer. One partner should make an offer. The other partner should give an uncertain answer. Respond with Let me know.**

LANGUAGE BOX			B	A
	A		**B**	**A**
Do you need ... Would you like ...	... any help with your project? ... anything to eat? ... any money to help with expenses?		I'm not sure. Not at the moment.	Well, let me know.

Listening 3: *Weather Forecast*

 1-17

A 🎧 **Listen to the weather forecast and fill in the blanks.**

Good **evening**. I **hope** you've been **enjoying** today's **warm weather**. Skies were partly ¹_____ in the **morning**, but those clouds **cleared** by **midday** and the temperature rose to **24 degrees** at **3** this **afternoon**. A light ²_____ from the **southeast** made conditions very **pleasant**. **Unfortunately**, the **warm** weather is **coming** to an **end** for now. Temperatures will **fall tomorrow**, **Tuesday**, as a **storm front** moves in from the **north**, bringing ³_____ in the **afternoon**. We're looking at a **maximum** of just **15 degrees** tomorrow. Those showers should **intensify** tomorrow **evening**, and will be accompanied by **strong northerly** ⁴_____. Severe **thunderstorms** are predicted for **Wednesday**, with a **high** of **13 degrees**. The **rainy weather** is expected to continue on **Thursday**, but should **ease** by the **end** of the **week**. **Sunny** ⁵_____ will return on **Friday**, in time for the **weekend**! A high of **21 degrees** is forecast for **Friday**, **23** for **Saturday**, and on **Sunday** we can expect a maximum of **25 degrees**. We're in for a **warm** and ⁶_____ weekend. I'll be back with **more** weather information at **nine** o'clock.

B 🎧 **Listen again. Circle T for true or F for false.**
1. The weather will change on Tuesday.   T / F
2. Stormy weather is expected to come from the north.   T / F
3. It will be fine on Wednesday.   T / F
4. The rainy weather will continue over the weekend.   T / F

Read the Forecast Aloud

Now pretend that you are a weather reporter. Read the forecast aloud. Include the words that you wrote to fill the blanks. Speak slowly and clearly. Use intonation—stress the important words (make them stronger). Practice by stressing the **bold** words in the weather forecast above. You may practice silently to yourself first. Then read the weather forecast aloud to a partner or to your class.

Education

Warm-up

A Different people undertake higher education for different reasons. What do you think is the purpose of higher education? Discuss your thoughts with a partner. Here are some ideas.

- To get the skills needed for a good job
- To develop a deep understanding of a specialized area of learning
- To develop a general understanding of how our world works
- To learn how to think independently and critically
- To interact with others who share a love of learning
- To achieve social status

B 👥 Universities and colleges generally offer a wide range of subjects. Work with a partner to group these subjects under the headings **sciences** or **humanities**.

biotechnology / linguistics / history / physics / molecular biology / philosophy / literature / chemistry

Sciences	Humanities

06

Listening 1

  CD 1-18

A 🎧 **Listen to the workshop presenter. Circle T for true or F for false.**

1. The workshop is on how to give effective presentations.   T / F
2. Before the coffee break, the workshop will cover notetaking at lectures.   T / F
3. "Cornell Notes" is a method of writing notes.   T / F
4. The presenter asks the students to open their textbooks.   T / F

B 🎧 **Listen again. Fill in the blanks.**

1. Good morning, everyone. Let's get _____.
2. The workshop is going to be broken up into two _____.
3. I've prepared a _____ that outlines what we'll be _____ today.
4. Remember this is a _____, not a lecture, and I'd like you all to _____.
5. Let me start by asking you a _____.

Tips for Communication

Introducing topics in the classroom

The presenter uses a variety of expressions to introduce ideas and information.
The topic of this morning's study skills workshop is ...
We're going to look at a number of ways to ...
In the first session we'll be focusing on ...
We're going to be talking about ...   I'm going to introduce you to ...

To move on to a new topic, a presenter or instructor might say:
Let's now turn to ...   I now want to take a look at ...
Let's move on to talk about ...

To recap something discussed earlier, a presenter or instructor might say:
Let's go back to our discussion of ...   Last time we were talking about ...
Coming back to what we were discussing yesterday ...

Listening 2

 1-19

A 🎧 Listen to Meg speaking with a building attendant on campus. Answer the questions.

1. Why did Meg go to Room 2C?
   a. to present a workshop   **b.** to attend a workshop   **c.** to write a report

2. Why was nobody in Room 2C?
   a. because the workshop was canceled   **b.** because the workshop was moved
   c. because Meg came on the wrong day

3. What was the problem in Room 2C?
   a. Too many people turned up.   **b.** The workshop started late.
   c. There was a problem with the computers.

B 🎧 Listen again. Fill in the blanks.

1. I've been waiting in Room 2C but nobody has _____ up.
2. There should have been a _____ on the door of Room 2C.
3. An email was sent out to everyone who _____ for the workshop.
4. It's downstairs on Level 1, beside the _____.

Talk with a Partner

👥 Practice talking about workshop venues and times. Choose a workshop from the list below. Take turns being the attendant and the student.

LANGUAGE BOX	
Attendant	**Student**
Hello. Can I help you?	I'm here to attend a workshop that's due to start at ... I've been waiting in ... but nobody has ...
Is that the ...?	Yes, it is.
There's been a change of venue. The workshop has been moved to ...	I'd better get to ... I've only got a couple of minutes!

Learning Support Center: Study Skills Workshops

Workshop title	Venue	Time
Time management	Room 2B	Monday 10 a.m.
Introduction to referencing	Room 2C	Monday 11 a.m.
Research skills	Library computer room	Monday 1 p.m.
Report writing	Room 2C	Monday 2 p.m.
Effective notetaking	Room 2B	Tuesday 10 a.m.
Academic writing	Room 1D	Tuesday 11 a.m.
Exam preparation	Room 2B	Wednesday 10 a.m.

Grammar Focus

Nobody, no one, nothing

Meg says to the building attendant: *I've been waiting in Room 2C but nobody has turned up.* In other words, there aren't any people there. Negative pronouns like *nobody* and *nothing* can be the subject of a sentence.
Nobody *lives in that old house.*   **Nothing** *will make me change my mind.*
A negative pronoun can also be the object of a sentence.
I have **nobody** *to talk to. Kevin ate* **nothing** *for breakfast.*
Nobody and *no one* mean the same thing and can be used interchangeably.
No one told me about the party. = **Nobody** *told me about the party.*

A Complete each sentence with **nothing** or **nobody** (or **no one**).

1. We all make mistakes. _____ is perfect!
2. Yesterday was very quiet. _____ happened!
3. The children ate all of the food. There's _____ left!

B Write one-word answers: **nothing** or **nobody** (or **no one**).

1. What's wrong? _____
2. Who were you speaking to a little while ago? _____
3. Who lives in the apartment upstairs? _____

Develop Your Speaking Skills

👥 Work in pairs and practice using **nothing** or **no one**. Look at the diary pages.

Monday 14 *Bowling with Jack 7 p.m.*		Thursday 17	
Tuesday 15		Friday 18	
Wednesday 16 *Dinner with Pete and Sue 7 p.m.*		Saturday 19 *Meet Jo 6 p.m.*	Sunday 20

A Practice the dialog.

A: What are you doing on Monday evening?
B: I'm going bowling with Jack.
A: Who are you seeing on Tuesday evening?
B: No one.

B Now ask and answer. Use the diary pages or create your own week.

LANGUAGE BOX	
A	**B**
What are you doing on ...?	I'm ... / Nothing.
Who are you seeing on ...?	Jack. / No one.

Listening 3: *Talk*

 CD 1-20

🎧 **Listen to the librarian's talk. Check the things the librarian mentions.**

1. books	☐	7. music	☐
2. journals	☐	8. computers	☐
3. e-books	☐	9. printers	☐
4. newspapers	☐	10. copiers	☐
5. inter-library loans	☐	11. scanners	☐
6. study rooms	☐	12. workshops	☐

Listening 4: *Voicemail*

CD 1-21

A 🎧 **Listen to the message. Circle the correct answer.**

What is the main reason for Meg's call to Charlie?

a. to apologize for being absent

b. to give him some information

c. to ask him to get some information for her

B 🎧 **Listen again and circle the correct answers.**

1. When is the term test?

    a. today   b. tomorrow   c. next week

2. What does Meg ask Charlie to pick up?

    a. a copy of any handouts   b. a copy of the test paper   c. her class notes

Speaking: *Leave a Voicemail Message*

👥 **Work with a partner. Take turns to practice leaving a voicemail message asking for a favor. Use expressions from the box. Use the different situations and favors.**

LANGUAGE BOX				
Hi, ... It's ... here. I'm not coming in to classes today because ...	I have a medical appointment. I have a job interview. I'm not feeling well.	Can I ask you to do me a favor? Could you ...	... let Mr. Costa know I'll bring my report in tomorrow? ... put my name on the list for the writing workshop? ... pick up a copy of any handouts for me? ... check what result I got in the term test?	Thanks!

Warm-up

A How do you get to know a new city after you arrive there? Read what these travelers say. Match their words to the pictures.

❝ I take a tour, either a bus tour or a guided walk. ❞ __

❝ I like to take a trip on a ferry. ❞ __

❝ I go for a long walk through the streets and parks, to get a feel for the place. ❞ __

❝ I look for a nice café, restaurant or bar where I can meet some locals. ❞ __

❝ I head straight for the major sights of the city. ❞ __

❝ I go for a run. I usually research a good route on the Internet before I arrive. ❞ __

B 👥 Talk with a partner. Which of these ideas would work best for you in a new city?

Listening 1

A 🎧 Bill has just arrived in Sydney and is asking how to get from Sydney Airport to the city center. Circle **T** for true or **F** for false.

1. The only way to get to the city center is by train.   T / F
2. You can use a credit card to travel on the train.   T / F
3. Rideshare to the city center will cost less than $50.   T / F
4. You can only buy an Opal card from a vending machine.   T / F

B 🎧 Listen again. Complete the information about the Sydney Airport train.

Sydney Airport to Central Station	
1	Train fare: $ _____
2	Trip time: _____ minutes
3	Departing from Platform _____
4	Departing every _____ minutes

Tips for Communication

Responding to more than one thing

The airport assistant says: *Hello. Welcome to Sydney. Can I help you?*

Bill replies: *Thanks, hi. Yes, can you tell me how to get from the airport to the city center?*

Notice how Bill is responding to three different things the assistant has said.

Welcome to Sydney—**Thanks**

Hello—**Hi**

Can I help you?—**Yes, can you tell me how to get from the airport to the city center?**

People often ask more than one question or say more than one thing at a time. It's okay to take your time when answering and respond to each thing.

A: *Good morning. I like your sunglasses. What can I get you?*
B: *Hi. Thanks! I'd like a cappuccino, please.*

A: *Hi, how are you? I'm Ella.*
B: *Hello, I'm Tony. I'm well, thanks, and you?*

07

Listening 2

🎧 1-23

A 🎧 Listen to Bill and his Australian friend Anna talking about going to the Sydney Opera House. Circle the correct words.

1. *The Magic Flute* is playing on **Wednesday and Friday** / **Thursday and Saturday** nights.
2. Bill wants to go and see *Carmen* / *The Magic Flute*.
3. Bill **can** / **can't** get a student discount on his opera ticket.
4. They will try to get cheaper seats at the **side** / **back** of the theater.
5. They want to go to the opera on **Thursday** / **Friday** night.

B 🎧 Listen again. Fill in the blanks.

1. Is it possible to go _____?
2. What's _____ at the Opera House?
3. Are the tickets _____?
4. Which night do you want to _____?
5. What time does it _____?

Talk with a Partner

👥 Practice talking with another student about going to see an opera at the Sydney Opera House. Choose from the box below. Ask about operas, nights, times, and prices.

LANGUAGE BOX

What's on at ...? I'd love to see an opera at ...
Which night ...?   What time ...?
How much are the tickets? They range from ... to ...

Opera performances, Sydney Opera House			
Date	Time	Opera	Ticket prices
Monday, May 3	7:30	Tosca	$48–$285
Tuesday, May 4	7:00	The Fairy Queen	$56–$290
Wednesday, May 5	8:00	Madam a Butterfly	$48–$285
Thursday, May 6	7:30	Tosca	$48–$285
Friday, May 7	8:00	Madam a Butterfly	$48–$285
Saturday, May 8	7:30	The Barber of Seville	$45–$270

34

Grammar Focus

Embedded "Wh" questions

Bill asks: *Can you tell me how to get from the airport to the city center?*

This is an example of an "embedded" question. We often use embedded questions to sound more polite. The question is preceded by a phrase such as *Can you tell me ...?, Could you tell me ...?,* or *Do you know ...?*

The question word (*where, how,* etc.) stays the same, but the word order of the question changes. Look at these examples:

Direct question	Embedded question
How much is the train fare?	***Do you know** how much the train fare is?*
How long is the train trip?	***Could you tell me** how long the train trip is?*
Where can I buy a ticket?	***Can you tell me** where I can buy a ticket?*
How can I pay?	***Could you tell me** how I can pay? (or **Could you tell me** how to pay?)*

Here are more examples with *does* or *did* in the direct question:

When does the next bus depart?	***Do you know** when the next bus departs?*
When did they arrive?	***Can you tell me** when they arrived?*

Change from direct to embedded questions using phrases from above.

1. Where is the Australian Museum? _____

2. Where do the ferries depart from? _____

3. How much is a ticket to the zoo? _____

4. What's the quickest way to Bondi? _____

Develop Your Speaking Skills

👥 **Work in pairs and practice asking for directions using embedded questions. Imagine one of you is a visitor to your own city.**

A **Practice the dialog.**

A : Can you tell me what the quickest way to the fish market is?
B : Sure. It's quickest to take the subway.
A : Thanks. Do you know where the nearest subway station is?
B : Yes, it's just around the corner.

B **Now ask and answer, using language from the box.**

LANGUAGE BOX		
A		**B**
Can you tell me ... Could you tell me ... Do you know ...	art museum palace park department store concert hall train station	Sure. It's ... Yes, you should ... Yes, there's a ...

Listening 3: *Announcement*

🎧 **CD** 1-24

A 🎧 Listen to the beach safety talk and fill in the blanks.

Welcome to **Sydney**. Our **beaches** are **great** places to visit and enjoy the **sun**, **surf**, and **sand**. But they can also be **dangerous**, **especially** if you aren't used to **swimming** in the ¹_____. **Swimmers** often need to be **rescued** from our beaches. And **sadly**, some people lose their **lives**.

So, **follow** these **safety tips** at the beach:

- **Swim** between the red and **yellow flags**. These **flags** are put in the sand to mark the ²_____ **area** for **swimming**, and **lifeguards** are on **patrol** there.

- Before you **enter** the water, **stop** and **think**—is it too ³_____? Conditions can **change quickly**. **Read** the **safety** signs.

- Don't go **swimming alone**. Swim with a ⁴_____.

- **Keep away** from **rips**. Rips are **strong currents** of **water flowing** out to **sea**, and they can carry **people** with them. You may be able to **identify** a rip from the **deeper**, **dark-green water**, with **clouds** of **sand** in it.

- If you **do** get into **difficulty** in the water, don't ⁵_____. **Don't** swim **against** a **rip**. Stay **calm**, **float**, and **raise** one **hand** so a **lifeguard** can see you need **help**.

Follow these **tips** for an **enjoyable** and **safe visit** to the **beach**.

B 🎧 Listen again. Write short answers to these questions.
1. What do the red and yellow flags show at the beach? _____
2. What is a rip? _____
3. How can you let a lifeguard know you need help in the water? _____

Read the Announcement Aloud

Now pretend that you are the speaker. Read the announcement aloud. Include the words that you wrote to fill the blanks. Speak slowly and clearly. Use intonation—stress the important words (make them stronger). Practice by stressing the **bold** words in the announcement above. You may practice silently to yourself first. Then read the announcement aloud to a partner or to your class.

Learning English

Warm-up

A Outside of classroom time, what strategies do you use to improve your English? Look at the list below. Check the strategies you use. Can you add any more to the list?

☐ Use a language-learning app

☐ Watch English-language movies

☐ Do crosswords and other word puzzles

☐ Write down new words and phrases in a notebook

☐ Search online for English language pronunciation sites

☐ Listen to English-language songs (and sing along with them)

☐ Read English-language books and magazines (silently or aloud)

☐ Study English grammar (books or websites) and do grammar exercises

☐ Find an English-speaking friend for conversation, face-to-face or on video calls

☐ Watch interviews with famous English-speaking people (actors, politicians, etc.)

☐ Have an "English-only" time, when you and your friends agree to speak only English

☐ Listen online to radio stations from the U.S., the U.K., or other English-speaking countries

B 👥 Which strategies are most useful for improving different language skills? Discuss your ideas with a partner.

C Match the words with the correct meanings.

1. assess	•	• the way to say a word
2. comprehension	•	• a way of doing something
3. essay	•	• the ability to do something well
4. pronunciation	•	• a piece of writing on a topic
5. skill	•	• to decide how good something is
6. spell	•	• understanding what something means
7. strategy	•	• to say a word more strongly than other words in a sentence
8. stress	•	• to write or say the letters of a word correctly

Listening 1

A 🎧 Listen to Takashi and Maria talking about learning English. Which skills do they each find easiest and hardest? Check.

		Reading	Writing	Listening	Speaking
Takashi	*easiest*	☐	☐	☐	☐
	hardest	☐	☐	☐	☐
Maria	*easiest*	☐	☐	☐	☐
	hardest	☐	☐	☐	☐

B 🎧 Listen again. Who mentions these strategies for improving English language skills? Write **T** for Takashi or **M** for Maria.

1. Read newspapers _____
2. Keep a note of new words and phrases _____
3. Read aloud _____
4. Listen to radio news _____
5. Write in a diary _____

Tips for Communication

Expressing difficulty
Takashi talks about listening to native English speakers and says: *I often have trouble keeping up.* Maria says: *Getting the grammar and spelling correct is a challenge.*

Here are some useful expressions for talking about things we find hard to do.

I often have trouble ... -ing ...	*I often have trouble using the correct form of a verb.*
I find it hard to ...	*I find it hard to give more than a short answer to people.*
I find it difficult to ...	*I find it difficult to know how formal or informal I should be.*
I find it tricky to ...	*I find it tricky to stress the right word in a sentence.*
It isn't easy to ...	*It isn't easy to understand what people are saying.*
For me, it's hard to ...	*For me, it's hard to pronounce certain consonants.*
I find ... a challenge.	*I find writing a challenge.*
... is / are challenging for me.	*Phrasal verbs are challenging for me.*

It's useful to be able to express difficulty. That way, you're more likely to get help from people!

Listening 2

🎧 1-26

A 🎧 Listen to a professor telling an English class about a test. Circle **T** for true or **F** for false.

1. Friday's test will have a listening section.   T / F
2. Each short reading text will have five comprehension questions.   T / F
3. The response to the email should be just one sentence.   T / F
4. The essay topic will be completely new for the students.   T / F
5. At the end of the term, the students will give presentations.   T / F

B 🎧 Listen again. Complete this summary of the test.

ENGLISH: Progress test

Reading section:

- Complete ten **1**_____

- Answer comprehension questions on **2**_____ short texts

3_____ **section:**

- Respond to an **4**_____   15 minutes

- Write an **5**_____ (approximately 300 **6**_____)   45 minutes

Talk with a Partner

👥 Takashi says: *I'm happy to help you with your grammar if you like.*

Practice expressing difficulty and offering to help. Choose one of the difficulties from the box below. Change the word forms if you need to.

A	B
LANGUAGE BOX	
I find it difficult to ...	I'm happy to help you with that if you like.
For me, it's hard to ...	Would you like me to help you with that?
I often have trouble ...	I could work with you on that if you like.
... is / are challenging for me.	
That would be great. Thanks.	

spelling, using phrasal verbs, pronunciation/pronouncing ..., writing, stressing the right word,

Grammar Focus

Find it + adjective + infinitive (with "to")

Maria says: *I find it hard to use exactly the right vocabulary.*

We can use the structure *find it + adjective + infinitive (with "to")* to express feelings about activities. The pronoun *it* refers to the activity described by the infinitive verb.

Here are more examples:
I ***find it useful to carry*** a pen with me wherever I go.
I ***find it relaxing to listen*** to music.
I ***find it easier to work*** early in the morning than late at night.

Write sentences with the structure *I find it + adjective + infinitive (with "to")*, using the following word prompts.

1. hard / study in a noisy place

   _____

2. interesting / hear different people's opinions about the news

   _____

3. difficult / know what Sam really thinks of me

   _____

4. helpful / organize my things for the next day before I go to bed at night

   _____

5. enjoyable / try cooking a new recipe from time to time

   _____

Develop Your Speaking Skills

👥 In "Talk with a Partner" on the previous page, you talked about things you find difficult about learning English. Now practice talking about the positives: things you find easy, enjoyable, or fun!

A Practice the dialog.

A : What do you find easy about learning English?
B : I find it easy to read English-language newspapers.
A : And what do you find enjoyable or fun?
B : I find it fun to listen to song lyrics and sing along with them. But I sometimes get them wrong!

B Now ask and answer.

LANGUAGE BOX	
A	**B**
What do you find easy about learning English? And what do you find enjoyable or fun?	I find it easy to ... I find it fun to ...

Listening 3: Short Talk

 1-27

A 🎧 **You are going to give a short talk on what you like and dislike about learning English. First, listen to the model talk below and fill in the blanks.**

Hello, I'm Takashi. I'm going to talk to you about what I like and dislike about learning English. Firstly, the things I [1]_____: I enjoy learning new words. I pick up new words and phrases all the time, especially while I'm [2]_____. In conversation, I'm not afraid to ask people to explain a new word to me. This makes me feel more [3]_____ about my English. Also, I like studying grammar. Some people don't like grammar, but I don't [4]_____ it. Secondly, what I don't like: I don't like giving [5]_____! It isn't easy to stand up and speak to a group of people. I get nervous and I worry about my pronunciation. But I know it's good [6]_____. So, to summarize: I like learning new words and studying grammar, and I don't like giving presentations.

B **Now think about what you like and dislike about learning English. Write your own short talk in the box below. You may use the words or phrases in the language box to help you.**

Follow the structure of the talk above: Begin with a topic sentence, and then introduce your "likes" with *Firstly*. Then talk about your "dislikes" with *Secondly*. Conclude with a short summary.

YOUR TALK

LANGUAGE BOX

Firstly, ...   Secondly, ...
I like ...   I enjoy ...
This makes me feel ...

I don't like ...   I often have trouble –ing ...
I find it hard / difficult to ...
I get ...

Some people don't like ..., but I don't mind it.
So, to summarize: I like ..., and I don't like ...

Money

Warm-up

A 👥 Are you good with money? What ways do you know to save it? Look at the list below. Check the strategies you use. Talk with a partner. Can you add any more to the list?

☐ Don't buy new clothes

☐ Cut out non-essentials like coffee from a café

☐ Buy grocery items in bulk to get a better price

☐ Keep track of what you are spending your money on

☐ Buy the cheaper brands of things in the supermarket

☐ Make a budget, so you can plan what you spend your money on

☐ Don't take taxis or rideshares— walk, cycle, or take public transportation

☐ Don't eat out in restaurants and cafés. Cook or prepare your meals at home

☐ Always make a shopping list before you go to the supermarket, and stick to it

☐ Ask your cell phone and Internet service providers to put you on a cheaper plan

B Match the words with the correct meanings.

1. deposit • • to take money out of your bank account

2. withdraw • • to put money into your bank account

3. lend • • extra money that you pay for borrowing an amount of money

4. borrow • • the money used in a country, for example yen, euro, or dollars

5. currency • • to get money from a bank or a person with a plan to pay it back

6. interest • • to let someone have some of your money, agreeing that they will pay it back

Listening 1

CD 1-28

A 🎧 **Listen to Bill explaining how he saved money for his trip to Australia. Check the strategies that he mentions.**

1. get a job ☐
2. don't take taxis or rideshares ☐
3. don't eat out in restaurants and cafés ☐
4. cut out non-essentials like coffee from a café ☐
5. always make a shopping list before you go to the supermarket ☐
6. buy the cheaper brands of things in the supermarket ☐
7. buy grocery items in bulk to get a better price ☐
8. don't buy new clothes ☐

B 🎧 **Listen again. Circle the correct words.**

1. Bill worked in **a café** / **a restaurant**.
2. He worked **full-time** / **part-time**.
3. Bill **cut down on** / **completely stopped** buying take-out coffee.
4. He bought **no** / **only a few** new clothes.
5. Bill saved for his trip in **eight** / **eighteen** months.

Tips for Communication

I bet, you bet

When Bill tells Jo about cutting down on coffee, she says: *I bet that was hard.* She means that she is sure it was hard, because she knows he loves coffee.

We can use *I bet (or I'll bet)* in an informal way to say we are very confident that something is true.
It's raining really heavily. I bet the traffic is going to be terrible.
A : *I'm thrilled about my new job.* B : *Yes, I'll bet you are. It's great news.*
Note : *You bet* can be used to express enthusiastic agreement.
A : *Will you come and watch me sing?* B : *You bet I will!*

09

Listening 2 1-29

A 🎧 **Listen to Bill talking with the clerk at a currency exchange store in Australia. Fill in the blanks.**

1. I'd like to change some U.S. _____ into Australian dollars.
2. How much would you like to _____?
3. May I see your _____, please?
4. How would you like your Australian _____?
5. Could you give me some _____, please?

B 🎧 **Listen again. Answer the questions.**

1. How much will Bill get in Australian currency? $_____
2. How many of each Australian note does Bill ask for?

$100	$50	$20	$10
____	____	____	____

3. How much will Bill get in coins? $_____

Talk with a Partner

👥 **Practice asking about exchanging currency. Choose currencies and amounts from the box below. Ask and answer.**

LANGUAGE BOX	
Clerk	**Traveler**
Can I help you?	Yes, I'd like to change some Japanese yen into ...
Certainly. How much would you like to exchange?	Twenty thousand yen.
Just one moment... Twenty thousand yen will buy you ...	Okay.
May I see your passport, please?	Sure. Here it is.
How would you like your ...?	Can I have ... fifties, ... twenties, ... tens, and the rest in coins?

Currencies and amounts

	¥20,000 will buy you ...
Canadian dollars	$242.50 (*242 dollars and fifty cents Canadian*)
Euro	€166.40 (*166 euro and forty cents*)
British pounds	£141.40 (*141 British pounds and forty pence*)
U.S. dollars	$182.20 (*182 dollars and twenty cents U.S.*)

44

Grammar Focus

Asking polite questions: *could, may* and *would*

When Bill talks with the clerk, their language is polite. They make requests using the modal verbs *may* and *could*.

May I see your passport, please? *Could you give me some fifties, please?*

These modals mean the same as *can* (*Can I ...? Can you ...?*), but they are more formal and sound more polite. In business or service situations, such as offices and stores, we are more likely to hear requests with *may* and *could*. *May* is a little more formal than *could*. Note that both *could **I*** and *could **you*** are possible, but only *may **I*** is possible (not *may you*).

Could I have your name, please? **Could you** wait a moment, please?	**May I** have your name, please? _____

A Change these imperatives to polite requests with **Could you ..., please?**

1. Wait over there. _____

2. Open the window. _____

3. Fill out this form. _____

4. Lend me your pen. _____

B Make these requests more polite by changing **can** to **could** or **may**. Where possible, use **may**. Otherwise, use **could**.

1. Can I try on this shirt? _____

2. Can you give me a few more minutes? _____

3. Can you close the door? _____

4. Can I see your identification? _____

Develop Your Speaking Skills

👥 Work in pairs and practice asking polite questions over the phone.

A Practice the two dialogs.

A : May I speak to Ron Kidd, please? B : Certainly. May I ask who's calling? A : Kim Bolton. B : Thank you. Could you hold the line, please?	A : May I speak to Sue Fox, please? B : She's not here right now. A : Could I leave a message for her? B : Of course. Could you wait a moment, please?

B Now ask and answer in pairs. One partner asks to speak to one of these people. The other responds, according to whether the person is in or out.

In the office	Gina May Ben Scott Steve Gibb Nell King		Not in the office	Tim Day Jean Law Sue Lang Paul Hunt

Listening 3: *Announcement*

CD 1-30

🎧 Listen to the financial advisor's talk. Complete the information on the chart.

The 50:30:20 rule: spending your after-tax income

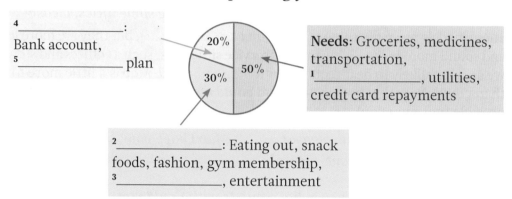

4_____:
Bank account,
5_____ plan

20%

50%

30%

Needs: Groceries, medicines, transportation,
1_____, utilities, credit card repayments

2_____: Eating out, snack foods, fashion, gym membership,
3_____, entertainment

Listening 4: *Voicemail*

CD 1-31

A 🎧 **Listen to the message. Circle the correct answer.**

Why is Pete calling Andy?

a. to ask Andy if he can borrow some money

b. to ask Andy to pay back some money

c. to tell Andy that he has bought some concert tickets

B 🎧 **Listen again and circle the correct answers.**

1. When does Pete want the money?

   a. in three weeks   b. in a day or two   c. today

2. How much does Pete want from Andy?

   a. $55   b. $60   c. $65

Speaking: *Leave a Voicemail Message*

👥 **Work with a partner. Take turns to practice leaving a voicemail message asking for a repayment. Use expressions from the box.**

LANGUAGE BOX
Hi ..., it's ... You remember I ...? I'm sorry to ask you this, but could you ...? I'd really appreciate it. The amount you owe me for your ticket is ... You can pay it directly into my bank account. Call me and I can give you my account details.

... paid for dinner / lent you ... / bought tickets for ...	$25	$55	$80	$35

The Environment

Warm-up

A News stories begin with a headline giving the main idea of the story. Match the news headlines to the pictures. Write the numbers of the pictures.

a. ___ **AIR QUALITY WARNING ISSUED FOR THIRD DAY**

b. ___ **THOUSANDS TURN OUT ACROSS CITY FOR TREE PLANTING DAY**

c. ___ **OIL SPILL CLEAN-UP "COULD TAKE MONTHS"**

d. ___ **NEW CONCERN OVER TOXIC LEAKS FROM LANDFILL SITE**

e. ___ **LAKE WATER QUALITY "BEST IN DECADES" AFTER CLEAN-UP PROGRAM**

f. ___ *New national park to be declared on edge of the city*

B 👥 Now read what these people are saying. Match the sentences to the pictures and headlines above.

❝I'm glad the forest is going to be preserved.❞

❝I'll come back often and see how this grows!❞

❝I find it difficult to breathe on days like this.❞

❝We won't be swimming there for a while!❞

❝It might be okay to start fishing there again.❞

❝I'm concerned that it will get into the groundwater.❞

Listening 1

 1-32

A 🎧 **Listen to Yoko talking with Marty on the phone. Circle T for true or F for false.**

1. Doing volunteer work for Greenbird is Yoko's idea.   T / F
2. Yoko has done volunteer work for Greenbird before.   T / F
3. Marty agrees to go with Yoko and help Greenbird.   T / F
4. The volunteers have to bring their own gloves.   T / F

B 🎧 **Listen again. Complete the details of the clean-up activity that Yoko and Marty will join.**

Minato Station clean-up activity	
Activity Date:	_____, April 4
Meeting time:	_____
Length of activity:	_____
Meeting place:	Main _____ of station
What to bring:	_____; we will supply gloves, _____, and tongs.
No need to register – just _____ up!	

Tips for Communication

Are you free? Are you doing anything?

Before Yoko asks Marty about going to the clean-up, she checks with him: *Are you free on Sunday?* He answers: *Yes, I am. Why?*

Here are some other ways to check if someone is free:
Are you doing anything on Sunday?   **Are you busy** on Sunday?
Do you have any plans for Sunday?

Note that if Marty is free, his answers to these questions would be *No*.
Are you doing anything on Sunday?   No, I'm not. Why?

But if Marty is busy on Sunday, his answers would be:
Are you free on Sunday?   No, I'm not.
Are you doing anything on Sunday?   Yes, I am.
Normally we would explain what we are doing:
Are you free on Sunday?   No, I'm not. I'm visiting my grandparents.

Listening 2

A 🎧 **Listen to Yoko and Dave. Answer the questions.**

1. What does Dave want to know?
   a. how to use his new phone
   b. what to do with his old phone
   c. what day the trash is collected
2. What did Dave do with the plastic envelope that he got?
   a. He posted it to the recycling company.
   b. He kept it.
   c. He threw it out.
3. What is Dave going to do with his old phone?
   a. He'll mail it to the phone recycling company.
   b. He'll put it into the trash.
   c. He'll take it to a phone store.

B 🎧 **Listen again. Fill in the blanks.**

1. I don't think it should just go into the _____.
2. Some of the materials in cell phones are _____.
3. Okay, but I can't put it in with plastic _____, can I?

Talk with a Partner

👥 Practice talking about taking part in events to help the environment. Person A, choose an event and call person B. Person B, ask questions.

TREE PLANTING MORNING
Riverside Park
Saturday, May 7. 9 A.M.–11 A.M.
Come and plant trees beside the river.
All welcome!

COMMUNITY GARDEN OPEN DAY
Angel Street Community Garden
Every Sunday, 1–5 P.M. Come along and do some weeding and watering at your local community garden. **Meet other gardeners!**

LANGUAGE BOX	
A	**B**
Are you free on ...? Are you doing anything on ...?	Yes. Why? No. Why?
Do you want to go and ... ... plant some trees ... ... do some gardening ...	What time ...? How long ...? Where ...?
It'll be ... We can ...	Let's do it. Sounds good.

Grammar Focus

Get + object + complement

When Yoko tells her friend Marty about helping to clean up the city, she says: *You don't have to get your hands dirty. Get your hands dirty* is an example of the structure verb + object + complement. The complement adds information about the object. In this case, the complement is an adjective. Here are more examples with get + object + adjective:

*When I go swimming, I don't like to **get my hair wet**.*

*It's six o'clock. I'll **get dinner ready** soon.*

A Complete the sentences with **get** or **got** and the given adjectives.

1. We need to _____ things _____ for tonight's party. (**ready**)
2. I'm sorry I _____ your name _____ earlier. (**wrong**)
3. What an amazing view! I'll _____ my camera _____. (**out**)
4. This advertisement is designed to _____ children more _____. (**active**)

Another verb commonly used in the verb + object + complement structure is *have*, with a past participle as the complement. We use this to talk about things that we ask other people to do for us. For example:

I'm having my hair cut this afternoon.   I had my carpet cleaned last week.

B Complete the sentences with **having** and the past participles of the given verbs.

1. George is _____ his car _____ today. (**service**)
2. They're _____ their house _____ this week. (**paint**)
3. I'm _____ these shoes _____ tomorrow. (**repair**)
4. We're _____ the old windows in our house _____. (**replace**)

Develop Your Speaking Skills

👥 **Work in pairs and practice talking about things you have done for you.**
Use questions with **have** or **get** and past participles. For example:

How often do you have your hair cut?   About once a month.

Where do you get it cut?   At the hair salon beside the library.

… your eyes tested?
… your blood pressure taken?
… your teeth checked?

Listening 3: *Short Talk*

 1-34

A 🎧 **You are going to give a short talk on what people can do to help the environment. First, listen to the model talk below and fill in the blanks.**

There are so many big environmental problems today, it's easy to think that you can't make a difference. But there are many small things you can do, and if everyone did them, it would make a big difference. I'm going to talk about three things you can do to ¹_____ the environment, and I'm sure you can think of others. Firstly, don't drink ²_____ water. Fortunately, we live in a country where water from the tap is perfectly safe to drink. There's no need to buy water in plastic bottles. That just creates more plastic ³_____ . Another thing you can do is to make sure your home is well insulated so that you don't use too much energy on ⁴_____. And finally, if you have a petrol or diesel car, don't make unnecessary ⁵_____ . Car-pool with other people. So, don't drink bottled water, insulate your home well, and reduce your car trips. These are three simple ways you can make a ⁶_____.

B **Now think about three more things we can do to help the environment. Write your own short talk in the box below. You may use the words or phrases in the language box to help you. You may use the ideas in the box below, or your own ideas.** Follow the structure of the talk above: Begin with a topic sentence, and then introduce your three goals with *Firstly, ... Another thing you can do is, ... Finally, ...* Conclude with a short summary.

YOUR TALK

LANGUAGE BOX

I'm going to talk about three things you can do to help the environment.
Firstly, ... Another thing you can do is ... And finally, ...

Don't ... Say no to ... Cut down on ...

Plant ... Switch off ... Unplug ... Use ... Fix ...

Things to think about:

electronic items / energy-efficient light bulbs / taps / trees / plastics (bags, straws, cups) / paper / printing / cars / public transportation

UNIT 11   *Clothes*

Warm-up

A 👥 **Where do you usually shop for clothes? Where do you like to shop most? Look at the list of places to shop for clothes and talk with a partner.**

- small clothing store or boutique
- department store
- discount store
- second-hand store (thrift shop, charity shop)
- online (on the Internet)

B **Which of the following best describes how often you shop for clothes?**

once or twice a year / every two or three months / once a month / maybe twice a month / once a week		

a. ☐ _____

b. ☐ _____

c. ☐ _____

d. ☐ _____

e. ☐ _____

f. ☐ _____

Listening 1

🎧 1-35

A 🎧 Meg and Alison are looking at shirts online. Listen and write the correct word for the pattern or fabric. Then number the pictures from 1 to 6 as you hear about each shirt.

checks	floral print	tartan	stripes	polka dots	denim

B 🎧 Listen again. Circle the correct words.

1. Alison is looking for a shirt for **summer** / **winter**.
2. Meg says that denim **can get hot** / **looks great**.
3. Alison decides to buy **one shirt** / **two shirts**.

Tips for Communication

The one, the ones
When Alison has narrowed her choice down to two shirts, she says: *It's out of the shirt with the floral print and the one with polka dots.* She uses the pronoun *one* instead of repeating the noun *shirt.* We often use the pronoun *one* (or *ones*) in this way. **A**: *Which dress do you like best?*   **B**: *The one with stripes.* **A**: *I love those black shoes.*   **B**: *I prefer the brown ones.*

Listening 2

 1-36

A 🎧 Listen to Meg speaking with a clothing store clerk. They are talking about two rain jackets. Check the correct boxes for each jacket.

	Jacket feature	Sedona	Corsica
1	Two-in-one: fleece inner lining and waterproof outer shell	☐	☐
2	Removable hood	☐	☐
3	Adjustable cuffs	☐	☐

B 🎧 Listen again. Fill in the blanks.

1. I want something in the _____ price range, I guess.
2. They're both excellent jackets and they're both reasonably _____.
3. The Corsica is a little _____ than the Sedona.
4. I'd like to _____ them on.
5. There's a _____ over there.

Talk with a Partner

👥 Practice shopping for clothes. Choose items from the box below. Take turns being the customer and the clerk.

LANGUAGE BOX	
Clerk	**Customer**
Hello. Can I help you? We have a lot of ... They're just over here. Take a look at this / these ... Sure. There's a mirror ... The fitting rooms are ...	Yes, I'm looking for a / some ... Something I can wear to /when ... I like this one / these ones ... Can I try it / them on?

hiking boots / rain jacket / short-sleeved shirt / light sweater / jeans

Grammar Focus

Linking verbs: *look, feel, smell, taste, seem* + adjective

When Meg is discussing shirts with her friend Alison, she says: *They look nice.* Used in this way, *look* is a linking verb (or "copular" verb). It links the subject, *they* (the shirts), with a word that describes the subject (*nice*). These verbs are followed by adjectives, not adverbs. Here are more examples:

*That soup **smells** good. Mr. Beatty **sounded** angry.*
*This sweater **feels** lovely and soft. Lee **seemed** upset about something.*

The linking verbs above describe how we perceive things with our senses. Note that some of these verbs can be used differently, not as linking verbs. In these examples, note the difference between the first and second instances of the verbs:

*Meg and Alison **looked** at the shirts. Alison said, "They **look** nice."*
*Rex **tasted** his coffee and then said, "This **tastes** terrible!"*

In each of the following sentences, is the bold verb a linking verb or not? Write L beside the linking verbs.

1. You **look** tired. Why don't you go and lie down? _____
2. Mmm! I can **smell** freshly baked bread. _____
3. This milk **smells** bad. I won't drink it. _____
4. I like to **taste** my meal before I put salt on it. _____
5. I just **felt** a drop of rain. Let's get inside. _____
6. This shirt **feels** uncomfortable on me. _____
7. Your new job **sounds** very interesting. _____

Develop Your Speaking Skills

👥 Work in pairs and practice talking about clothes you are trying on in a store.

A Practice the dialog.

A : How does this shirt look on me?
B : It looks great. How does it feel?
A : It feels very comfortable.

B Now ask and answer. Use clothing items and phrases from the box.

LANGUAGE BOX	
A	**B**
How does this ... look on me? It feels ...	It looks ... How does it feel?
Items	**Adjective**
shirt / sweater / jacket / denim	great / good / okay / cool / lovely / small / nice / comfortable / too tight

Listening 3: *Advertisement*

 1-37

A 🎧 **Listen to the advertisement and fill in the blanks.**

For **this** weekend only, **MyMart** is having a super ¹_____ on **men's** and **women's apparel**. There are **great** specials on **women's** apparel—with up to **70 percent** off **dresses, skirts,** ²_____, and **shoes**. And there are **fantastic** deals on men's apparel—with up to **50 percent** off **suits, shirts,** and ³_____; and up to **60** percent off **polo shirts, casual pants,** and ⁴_____. This **weekend, get** to **MyMart** for **top-quality apparel** at **amazing prices**. Shop **in store** or ⁵_____, with **two** to **four days delivery**. The **Super Weekend Sale** at **MyMart**. Sale starts **Friday** at **4 p.m**. and ends ⁶_____ at **7 p.m**.

B 🎧 **Listen again. Answer to these questions.**

1. Which department of MyMart is offering the biggest discounts—women's apparel or men's apparel? _____

2. In men's apparel, which has the bigger discounts—business wear or casual wear? _____

3. What are the two ways of shopping in the sale? _____

4. Over how many days will the sale be held? _____

Read the Advertisement Aloud

Now pretend that you are the announcer. Read the advertisement aloud. Include the words that you wrote to fill the blanks. Speak slowly and clearly. Use intonation—stress the important words (make them stronger). Practice by stressing the **bold** words in the script above. You may practice silently to yourself first. Then read the advertisement aloud to a partner or to your class.

Buildings and Addresses

Warm-up

A Match the words to the pictures.

1. ☐

2. ☐

3. ☐

4. ☐

5. ☐

a. elevator   b. escalator

c. basement

e. reception   d. staircase

f. main entrance

g. arcade   h. ramp

6. ☐

7. ☐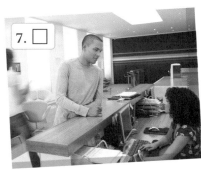

8. ☐

B Use words from above to complete these sentences.

1. Park your car in the _____ and then come up and speak to someone at _____.

2. Unfortunately, the _____ is not working today. You'll have to come up the stairs to Level 6.

3. There's a nice shopping _____ that runs between Second Street and Third Street.

Listening 1

A 🎧 **Bill is on the phone, asking for directions to an office. Listen and circle T for true or F for false.**

1. Bill is meeting someone in a travel company.   T / F
2. Bill wants to get a job in the office.   T / F
3. The office is close to a train station.   T / F
4. Bill says he wants to go shopping on the way to the office.   T / F
5. Bill can take the elevator up to the office.   T / F

B 🎧 **Listen again. Fill in the blanks.**

1. It takes about _____ minutes to walk to the office from Town Hall Station.
2. When he comes to Kent Street, he will turn _____.
3. The office is on the _____ floor.
4. Bill needs to talk to someone at reception on the _____ floor.
5. Bill will go up to the office by the _____.

Tips for Communication

Ground floor or first floor?

The receptionist says: *Go to reception on the ground floor and they'll show you where the stairs are.* The building's reception is on the same level as the street.

In some countries, such as Australia, New Zealand, and the U.K., the street level of a building is called the *ground floor*, or *Ground Level*. The floor one up from this is called the *first floor*, or *Level 1*.

Come in the front entrance and take the escalator up to the first floor.

In other countries, such as the United States, the floor at street level is called the *1st floor*, or *Level 1*.

I'll meet you in the café just inside the main entrance on Level 1.

Listening 2

🎧 1-39

A 🎧 **A member of the public is calling a museum. Listen and circle the correct answer.**

1. What does the caller want to know?
   a. how to get to the museum
   b. what people can see in the museum
   c. how people in a wheelchair can access the museum
2. If you are using the museum's rear entrance, what do you have to do?
   a. come up a flight of stairs
   b. press a button to be let in
   c. come up a ramp
3. How many levels of the museum are there?
   a. one   b. two   c. three
4. How will the customer travel to the museum?
   a. by taxi   b. by private car   c. by train

B 🎧 **Listen again. Check the parts of the building that are mentioned in the phone call.**

1. front entrance ☐
2. reception ☐
3. rear entrance ☐
4. elevators ☐
5. offices ☐
6. restrooms ☐
7. gallery rooms ☐
8. café ☐
9. gift shop ☐

Talk with a Partner

👥 Practice asking for directions over the phone. Choose addresses and locations from the box below.

LANGUAGE BOX

A	B
Can you give me directions to your office, please?	Sure. We're just a ...-minute walk from Central Station. Come out of the station at Exit number ... Turn ... on ... Street and walk about ...meters.
You're at ..., right?	Yes, we're on the ... floor.
Thanks very much.	

Level 3, 620 Lake Street
100 meters from Central Station / Exit number 2 / two-minute walk

Level 10, 400 Market Street
250 meters from Central Station / Exit number 4 / three-minute walk

Grammar Focus

Verb + object + infinitive (with "to")

The caller to the museum says: *I'll get the driver to drop me off at the main entrance.* Used in this way, *get* means to instruct, ask, or persuade. We use the structure *verb + object + infinitive (with "to")* to describe people saying things that cause other people to take actions. Here are more examples, with *get*.

I'll **get the waiter to bring** another spoon.
Don't try to move that sofa by yourself. **Get someone to help** you.

Here are more examples, with other verbs commonly used in this way:

I **asked Phil to buy** a bottle of soda water.
Please **remind me to call** my mom after lunch.
The teacher **told the students to open** their books.
The sergeant **ordered the soldiers to stand** to attention.
I was going to stay home, but my friends **persuaded me to go out** with them.

Describe what happened by completing the sentences with *object* + *infinitive* (with "to").

1. "Turn right, please driver."   He asked _____

2. "Class, stop talking."   The teacher told _____

3. "Don't forget to vote, Jim."   Sara reminded _____

4. "Passengers, please fasten   The captain told _____
   your seat belts."

Develop Your Speaking Skills

Work in pairs and practice the dialog.

A Practice the dialog.

A : Excuse me, the light in the store room has gone out.
B : Okay. I'll get the building manager to replace the light bulb.
A : Thanks very much.
B : Thank you for letting me know.

B Now ask and answer. One partner should mention a problem. The other should respond by saying they will get someone to do something about it.

LANGUAGE BOX	
Excuse me ...	Okay. I'll get a ... to ...
... the elevator is not working.	technician / glazier / plumber / cleaner / repair / replace / mop up ...
... there's a broken window Room 4.	
... a faucet in the kitchen is leaking.	Thank you for letting me know.
... there's water on the floor of the hall.	

1-40

Listening 3: Announcement

🎧 A fire warden's job is to take control if there's a fire and make sure everyone is safe. Listen to the fire warden's talk. Complete the summary.

Building evacuation procedure

You will need to evacuate the building if:

- you hear the fire ^{1}_____; or
- you are told to evacuate by a fire ^{2}_____.

Leave the building in a calm manner. Give help to others if needed. In case of fire, do not use the ^{3}_____. Make your way to street level via the main ^{4}_____ or via the fire stairs at the ^{5}_____ of the building. Gather at the assembly point ^{6}_____ Clay Street in Jackson Park. Wait there for a fire warden or safety officer.

Listening 4: Voicemail

 1-41

A 🎧 Listen to the message. Circle the correct answer.

Why is Shauna calling Bill?

    a. to invite him for dinner

    b. to ask for directions to Bill's place

    c. to give Bill her address

B 🎧 Listen again and circle the correct answers.

    1. What is the apartment number?
       a. 805   **b.** 809   **c.** 829

    2. What time is the invitation for?
       a. 6:30   **b.** 7:00   **c.** 7:30

Speaking: Leave a Voicemail Message

👥 Work with a partner. Take turns to practice leaving a voicemail message telling someone how to get to your place. You may use your own address or make one up. Use expressions from the box.

LANGUAGE BOX

Hi ..., it's ...
I'm calling to give you my address.
I'm / We're at ...   I'm / We're in apartment ...
Take the elevator to ... / Come up the stairs to ...
See you tomorrow evening at ...
You have my number. Call me if you have any problems getting here.

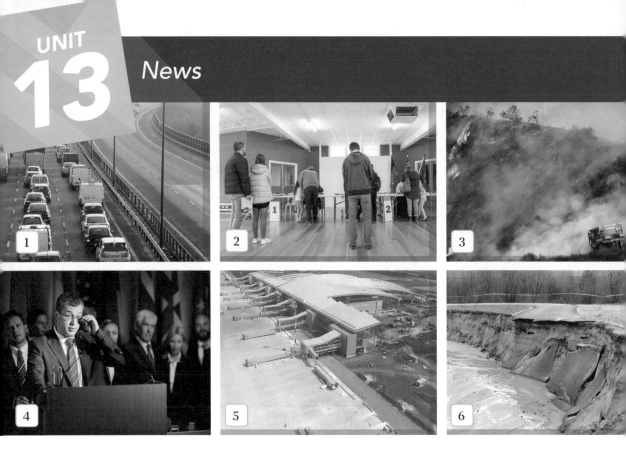

Warm-up

A Read the news headlines and match them to the pictures. Write the numbers of the pictures.

a. ___

FLOOD DAMAGE CAUSES ROAD CLOSURES

b. ___

VOTING BEGINS IN EASTERN STATES

c. ___

WILDFIRES THREATEN THOUSANDS OF HOMES

d. ___

FOUR-VEHICLE ACCIDENT CAUSES LONG DELAYS ON M7

e. ___

INTERNATIONAL TALKS CLOSE WITH NO AGREEMENT ON TRADE

f. ___

Construction underway on airport terminal expansion

B 👥 Work with a partner. Talk about what might be happening in each news story. Which area of news do you generally find most interesting?

Listening 1

 1-42

A 🎧 Listen to Takashi and Beth talking about a news story. Number the sentences below from **1** to **8** to show the correct order.

a. ____ The car stopped.

b. ____ The floodwaters rose.

c. _1_ The car drove into floodwaters.

d. ____ A police helicopter spotted the car.

e. ____ The people in the car climbed onto the roof.

f. ____ The people were interviewed for the TV news.

g. ____ The people tried to phone for help but had no signal.

h. ____ The Emergency Rescue Service came to help the people.

B 🎧 Listen again. Answer the questions.

1. On which day did the rescue happen? _____

2. How many people were in the car? _____

3. For how many hours did the people stay on the car roof? _____

4. What did the Rescue Service use to reach the people? _____

5. What did the police say you should never do? _____

Tips for Communication

It sure is
Takashi says: *This weather is wild, isn't it?* Beth replies: *It sure is!*
Takashi says: *Those people were lucky.* Beth replies: *They sure were.*
Beth's replies are both examples of using *sure* to express strong agreement.
This is stronger than if Beth just said: *Yes, it is* or *Yes, they were.*
The pattern is **pronoun** + **sure** + **verb**. Here are more examples:

	Sentence	Strong agreement
Main verb 'to be'	*Those fires in Australia* **are** *bad.*	*They sure are.*
	She **is** *an impressive politician.*	*She sure is.*
Main verb other than 'to be'	*The traffic* **moves** *slowly during rush hour.*	*It sure does.*
	He **spoke** *well.*	*He sure did.*
Auxiliary verb	*The weather* **can** *change quickly.*	*It sure can.*
	The Eagles **have** *started their season strongly.*	*They sure have.*

Listening 2

 1-43

A 🎧 A reporter is interviewing the chief medical officer of a new hospital. Listen and circle the correct answer.

1. What happened six years ago?

   a. Planning for the hospital started.

   b. The old children's hospital closed.

   c. There were delays in the construction of the hospital.

2. What will happen on Thursday?

   a. The building will be completed.

   b. Equipment and supplies will be moved into the hospital.

   c. The patients will be moved into the hospital.

3. How many beds will the new hospital have?

   a. 215   **b.** 216   **c.** 230

B 🎧 Listen again. Fill in the blanks.

1. It's a lot more _____ than the old children's hospital.

2. It's equipped with the most _____ medical technology.

3. Kids, parents, and medical staff all helped our architects to _____ this building.

4. There's also an outdoor play area on the _____.

Talk with a Partner

👥 Practice discussing news stories. Choose one of the stories below. You can make up some details about the story.

LANGUAGE BOX	
A	**B**
Did you see ... on the news? It happened on ... / in ... It ... / They ... / She ... / He ...	No, I didn't see that. What happened? How many ...? When ...? Where ...? Who ...? Why ...? How ...?

TRAIN DERAILS: FIVE INJURED
- Inter-city express
- Monday morning
- Traveling too fast
- Three carriages came off tracks
- 5 people hurt; no one killed

HIKER FOUND ALIVE
- Went for day-walk in wilderness area
- Didn't return, got lost, broke ankle
- Reported missing by family
- Rescuers searched for 11 days
- Found in cave; ate only chocolate

Grammar Focus

See someone –ing

Beth asks Takashi: *Did you see the people being rescued from the top of their car?*

She is asking him if he saw the rescue as it happened. We can guess that TV news cameras filmed it, perhaps from a helicopter.

We use the structure *verb + noun + present participle* when we are talking about actions that are in progress when we observe them. Verbs commonly used with this structure are *see*, *hear*, and *notice*.

Here are more examples:

*I **saw John running** in the park this morning.*
*Can you **hear the band playing** in the hall?*
*Did you **notice anybody behaving** suspiciously?*
*I **saw someone being** arrested by the police yesterday.*

Complete each sentence with a verb from the box. Use the present participle.

try	wait	bark	fly	have

1. I lay awake all night listening to a dog _____.
2. I saw someone _____ to break into a store, so I called the police.
3. I heard the people next door _____ an argument last night.
4. I live near the airport and always hear planes _____ overhead.
5. I saw Ben _____ at the bus stop, so I stopped my car and offered him a lift.

Develop Your Speaking Skills

👥 Work in pairs and practice talking about things you can hear or see.

A Close your eyes and don't speak. Be quiet and just listen for about thirty seconds. What can you hear? Try to hear four different things. Then tell your partner what you could hear.

For example:
I could hear a bus or truck going past in the street.
I could hear the clock ticking.

B Now try to remember the people and things you saw in the street this morning. Tell your partner what you saw.

For example:
I saw a woman selling flowers at a stall.
I saw some workers digging up the road.

Listening 3: Traffic Report

🎧 1-44

A 🎧 Listen to the traffic report and fill in the blanks.

I'm Sam **Barker**, reporting from the **5 News traffic helicopter**. Let's take a **look** at today's ¹_____ **commute**.

There are **heavy delays** on the **M6**, **northbound**, with **two** lanes ²_____. That's due to a **three-vehicle accident** earlier. **Traffic** is at a **standstill** up all the way **back** to **Eastern Creek**. If you're **headed** for the ³_____, think about **taking** an **alternative route** via **Elkhorn Road**.

Expect **delays** also on **Hills Drive westbound**, due to ⁴_____ at the **Grady** Street **intersection**.

And there's a **bus breakdown** on **Riverside Boulevard** near **Seventh Avenue**, causing some **delays** to eastbound ⁵_____.

Elsewhere across the city, **traffic** is generally moving **freely**. This is **Sam Barker**. I'll be **back** in **half** an **hour** with another ⁶_____. Drive **safely**!

B 🎧 Listen again. Circle T for true or F for false

1. Traffic going north on the M6 is moving very slowly.   T / F
2. An accident is causing delays at the intersection of Hills Drive and Grady Street.   T / F
3. On Riverside Boulevard a bus broke down going east.   T / F
4. The whole city is experiencing traffic delays.   T / F

Read the Traffic Report Aloud

Now pretend that you are the reporter. Read the traffic report aloud. Include the words that you wrote to fill the blanks. Speak slowly and clearly. Use intonation—stress the important words (make them stronger). Practice by stressing the **bold** words in the script above.

You may practice silently to yourself first. Then read the traffic report aloud to a partner or to your class.

Jobs and Work

Warm-up

A 👥 Look at the list of part time jobs. What do you think the duties of these jobs are? Match the duties in the box to the jobs. Some duties may go with more than one job. Talk with a partner.

Jobs	Duties
Tutor Waiter Amusement park staff Store assistant Mover	Show people where to go Stock shelves, keep aisles neat Greet and help customers Explain things clearly Remember what people asked for Stay on your feet for a long time Plan lessons Operate cash register Communicate well on phone Move furniture and equipment Greet people and check bags Check that equipment is safe

B Now read what these people are saying. Match them to their jobs.

"That's 17 dollars and 60 cents, thank you very much."

"Now, stay seated throughout the ride, with your seatbelts on. Have fun!"

"Here we go. The eggs ... and the pasta."

"Now, let's start by checking your homework from last week."

"Where would you like us to put the television?"

Listening 1

 1-45

A 🎧 Listen to Meg asking about a job she saw advertised. Circle the correct words in Meg's questions.

1. Can you tell me what the job **involves** / **requires**?
2. Do you need any **coaching** / **training** to do the job?
3. Are the jobs full-time or **casual** / **part-time**?
4. How do I **go** / **apply** for the job?

B 🎧 Listen again. Complete the notes that Meg took during the call.

Wait staff job at Astor Event Staffing
Called Monday morning, spoke to Andrew
Serving at weddings, celebrations and also corporate [1]_____
Duties:
   Setting up the [2]_____
   Laying [3]_____
   Serving food and beverages to [4]_____
   Clearing [5]_____
   Packing up after event has [6]_____
Training:
   Must have Food Handler [7]_____
   Can do training and get card [8]_____
   Costs [9]_____
Times:
   Can work just on weekends or throughout the [10]_____
How to apply:
   Apply online. After getting email, send [11]_____
   May be invited to group [12]_____

Tips for Communication

Asking about jobs

In exercise A above, there are some examples of questions to ask to find out about jobs.

Here are some more useful questions that you could ask:

Do you need any experience for this job?

Do you need any qualifications for the job?

What are the hours?

Are the working hours flexible?

Where is the job located?

How much does the job pay? / What's the rate of pay?

Can you tell me about the day-to-day duties of the job?

Can you tell me more about the conditions of the job?

Are there any opportunities for promotion in this job?

Listening 2

🎧 1-46

A 🎧 **Meg is at a job interview. Listen and circle T for true or F for false.**

1. Meg wants to work full-time.   T / F
2. Meg has worked in a store before.   T / F
3. Meg says she's good at interacting with people.   T / F
4. Meg can work all day on Wednesday.   T / F
5. The manager offers Meg a job.   T / F

B 🎧 **Listen again. Answer the questions.**

1. How many hours of work does Meg want to do per week? _____
2. How long are the weekend shifts at the store? _____
3. When does the manager ask Meg to start? _____
4. What is the first thing Meg will do on her first shift? _____
5. What color clothing does the manger ask her to wear? _____
6. Who will Meg work with to begin with? _____

Talk with a Partner

👥 Practice being in a job interview. You can use one of the jobs from the first three pages of this unit, or think of a different job.

A	B
LANGUAGE BOX	
What attracted you to working here at …?	I need … / I like … / I think this job …
Do you have any experience working in …?	I worked in …
Why did you finish that job?	Because …
In this job you'd need to …	That'd be okay. / I think I'm pretty good at … / I like …
How do you feel about …	
What hours are you interested in workng?	I'm looking for … / I could work …
Do you have any questions?	Yes. What …? / How much …? / When …?
I'm pleased to say I can offer you a job here.	Oh, that's great. Thanks.
Can you start tomorrow?	Yes, definitely.

Grammar Focus

Questions with the question word as subject

The store manager asks Meg: *What attracted you to working here at our store?* In this question, the question word *What* is the subject. A very simple, direct answer to the question could be something like: *The excellent pay attracted me.* But we often give more complex answers to questions, as Meg does: *Well, I need a part-time job, and I like the idea of working in retail.*

Here are more examples of questions with the question word as subject:

Q : What brings you here today?   **A :** *I'm keen to work for your company.*

Q : What took you so long to get here?   **A :** *My bus got stuck in traffic.*

Q : What motivates you in your work?   **A :** *I really like helping people.*

Q : Who phoned earlier?   **A :** *Maria Bezos. She wants you to call her.*

Write What or Who to begin these questions.

1. _____ wrote this report?
2. _____ sent you this letter?
3. _____ is your favorite movie?
4. _____ happened?
5. _____ asked you to come here today?
6. _____ gets you excited about your job?
7. _____ makes you think I can't cook?
8. _____ is coming to the meeting?

Develop Your Speaking Skills

👥 **Work in pairs and talk about the jobs or kind of work you would most like to do in the future. Use questions with the question word as subject.**

For example:

What area of work interests you the most?

What gets you excited?

What gives you satisfaction?

What motivates you?

What stresses you?

What makes you get out of bed in the morning?

Who inspires you?

Listening 3: *Induction Talk* 1-47

🎧 Listen to the welcome or induction talk for new employees at a company. Complete the notes from the talk.

Wear your security pass around your neck ¹_____.
Fill out the forms to get yourself into the system and onto the
²_____.
Read the company policies document for information including:
- ³_____ code
- how to report in if you are ⁴_____

Meet your ⁵_____! They will:
- answer questions and help you settle in
- take you on a ⁶_____

Listen to Bobby talk about activities organized by the ⁷_____

Listening 4: *Voicemail* 1-48

A 🎧 Listen to the message. Circle the correct answer.
Why is Meg calling Hugo?
a. to ask Hugo if she and he can swap work shifts on the weekend
b. to tell Hugo that she can work some extra hours on the weekend
c. to ask Hugo if he knows when they are both rostered to work

B 🎧 Listen again and circle the correct answers.
1. What does Meg want to do on Sunday evening?
   a. work   b. arrange a party at work   c. attend a family party
2. What does Meg ask Hugo to do?
   a. call or text her with his answer   b. call Mr. Turner for her
   c. meet her at work

Speaking: *Leave a Voicemail Message*

👥 Work with a partner. Take turns to practice leaving a voicemail message asking for a favor from a work colleague. Use expressions from the box.

LANGUAGE BOX

Hi ... This is ... from work.
I'm wondering if you can ...
... tell the manager I'm running ten minutes late. The bus / train ...
... swap a shift with me. I'm supposed to ... but ...
... tell me what times I'm rostered this week. I can't get onto the app ...

I could ...
Please call or text to let me know. / I'd really appreciate it.

UNIT 15

Future Plans

| travel | relationship | family | career | home |
| study | health | purchases | business | finance |

Warm-up

A Do you have plans or goals for your future? Think about the areas in the box. Write some things that you aim to do in the following time periods.

In the next month	_____
In the next 6 months	_____
In the next year	_____
In the next 5 years	_____
In the next 15 years	_____

B 👥 Compare your answers with a partner. Tell your partner about your plans.

72

Listening 1

 1-49

A 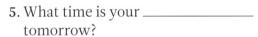 **Takashi is going back to Japan. Listen to Maria and Takashi saying goodbye. Circle T for true or F for false.**

1. Takashi thinks his overseas study has been good for him.   T / F
2. Takashi still feels shy and nervous talking to people in English.   T / F
3. Takashi will start studying as soon as he gets back to Japan.   T / F
4. Maria offers to drive Takashi to the airport.   T / F

B 🎧 **Listen again. Fill in the blanks.**

1. I can't believe you're _____ back to Japan tomorrow!
2. It seems like only _____ that you arrived here!
3. Has coming here to study been _____?
4. What are your _____ for the future after you get back to Japan?
5. What time is your _____ tomorrow?

Tips for Communication

Saying goodbye

Maria and Takashi are saying goodbye after studying together for six months. Here are some of the expressions they use:

It's been wonderful to meet you.
Thanks for all your support and encouragement.
I really hope we can stay in touch. / Let's keep in touch.
I'll miss you. Take care.

Here are some more "saying goodbye" expressions:

It's been great / so nice to meet you.
I've really enjoyed getting to know you.
Thanks for all your help / for taking care of me / for everything.

Note that when Maria says: *It's been wonderful to meet you, Takashi*, he answers: *Likewise, Maria.*

This is a way of saying *I feel the same way toward you.*

Listening 2

 1-50

A 🎧 Maddie wants to be a film maker. Listen and check the things she is doing or planning to do to advance her career.

1. ☐ making her own films
2. ☐ learning film-making skills online
3. ☐ helping out with other people's projects
4. ☐ getting experience
5. ☐ expanding her network / building up her contacts
6. ☐ buying the best gear
7. ☐ applying for film school

B 🎧 Listen again. Circle the correct words.

1. Maddie has made a couple of **short** / **full-length** films.
2. Recently Maddie has done some **paid** / **unpaid** work on some film projects.
3. Maddie shot her first film on **her phone** / **a camera she borrowed**.
4. In the future, Maddie wants to make **comedies** / **documentaries**.

Talk with a Partner

👥 Practice talking about future career plans. Ask and answer.

LANGUAGE BOX	
A	**B**
I hear you want to be a ... Tell me about it.	Yes, I ... I've made ... / I like ... I'd like to make a career out of it.
How do to you plan to do that? What about professional training? What qualifications do you need? Do you have to ...? What kind of ...? Good luck with it!	I'm expanding ... / building up ... I'd like to do

Grammar Focus

It's been wonderful: present perfect + adjective

Maria says: *It's been wonderful to meet you, Takashi.* In this sentence, the pronoun *it* refers to the action described by the infinitive verb: *to meet you.* If Maria was talking about the present, she might say: *It is nice to meet you.* But Maria is referring to the time since Takashi arrived up until the present, so she uses the present perfect: *It has been wonderful.*

Here are more examples of this *It + present perfect + adjective* structure:
It's been good *to become more confident in speaking English.*
It's been interesting *to learn about the way of life in this country.*
It's been fun *to go out and meet so many new people.*
It's been difficult *to be so far away from my home.*

Here are examples of *present perfect + adjective* with other subjects:
I'm sorry I haven't called you lately. **I've been busy**.
Thanks for all your help. **You've been very kind** *to me.*

Complete the sentences with present perfect (has/have been) and the given adjectives.

1. I haven't attended class all week. I _____. (**unwell**)
2. He _____ to play the violin since he was five. (**able**)
3. I feel sleepy. I _____ since 4:30 a.m. (**awake**)
4. Thanks for explaining it to me. You _____. (**helpful**)
5. It _____ to watch the World Cup every day on TV. (**exciting**)

Develop Your Speaking Skills

👥 Work in pairs and practice looking back over a time that you have shared.

A Practice the dialog.

A : Thanks for all your help over the past six months. You've been very kind.
B : You're welcome. It's been great to meet you. Let's keep in touch.
A : I'd like that. Take care!

B Now ask and answer. Use expressions from the box.

LANGUAGE BOX		
A		**B**
Thanks for ... over the past ... your support / all your help / taking care of me / everything you've done	You've been ... so kind / very helpful / really generous	You're welcome. It's been ... great / terrific / nice ... to meet you.

Listening 3: *Short Talk*

 1-51

A 🎧 **You are going to give a short talk on personal goals. First, listen to the model talk below and fill in the blanks.**

I've decided to set myself three personal goals for the next six months. Firstly, I'm going to ¹_____ a gym. There's a gym close to where I live, so it's easy for me to get to. I'll aim to attend fitness classes there ²_____ times a week. This should really help me to improve my fitness. Secondly, I want to learn how to cook some new dishes. I can cook a little but I'd like to be better at it. So I'll find some new ³_____ and try them out. And finally, I'd like to work on improving my punctuality. I always seem to arrive ⁴_____ for things and I don't like it. I know it can annoy my friends. So I'm determined to do better. I just need to start getting ready for things ⁵_____. So at the end of six months, I'd like to see these ⁶_____: being fitter, cooking more interesting things, and no more arriving late for things!

B **Now think about three personal goals that you could set for yourself for the next six months. Write your own short talk in the box below. Use the words and phrases in the language box to help you. You may use the ideas in the box below, or your own ideas.**

Follow the structure of the talk above: Begin with a topic sentence, and then introduce your three goals with Firstly, ... Secondly, ... Finally, ... Conclude with a short summary.

YOUR TALK

LANGUAGE BOX

I've decided to set myself three personal goals for the next six months.
Firstly, ... Secondly, ... And finally, ...
I'm going to ... I want to ... I'd like to work on improving ... I'll aim to ...
I'm determined to ... This should help me to ... I'd like to be better at ...
So, at the end of six months, I'd like to see these outcomes: ...

travel, read more books, have more 'alone' time, get a job, take up a hobby, improve my punctuality, save money, do some volunteer work, start a blog, join a sports club, have a medical checkup, keep a diary, take up swimming, have more family time, take up running, improve my grades

TEXT PRODUCTION STAFF

edited by	編集
Yasutaka Sano	佐野 泰孝
Minako Hagiwara	萩原 美奈子

English–language editing by	英文校閲
Bill Benfield	ビル・ベンフィールド

cover design by	表紙デザイン
Nobuyoshi Fujino	藤野 伸芳

text design by	本文デザイン
ALIUS(Hiroyuki Kinouchi)	アリウス（木野内 宏行）

CD PRODUCTION STAFF

narrated by	吹き込み者
Chris Koprowski (AmerE)	クリス・コプロスキ（アメリカ英語）
Karen Haedrich (AmerE)	カレン・ヘドリック（アメリカ英語）
Josh Keller (AmerE)	ジョシュ・ケラー　（アメリカ英語）
Jennifer Okano (AmerE)	ジェニファー・オカノ（アメリカ英語）

Listen Up, Talk Back Book 2 —English for Everyday Communication—
聞いて話せる英語演習 Book 2 —頻出表現で学ぶ実用英語—

2021年1月20日　初版発行
2024年3月15日　第5刷発行

著　者　James Bean
　　　　鎌倉　義士

発 行 者　佐野 英一郎
発 行 所　株式会社 成 美 堂
　　　　　〒101-0052　東京都千代田区神田小川町3-22
　　　　　TEL 03-3291-2261　FAX 03-3293-5490
　　　　　https://www.seibido.co.jp

印刷・製本　萩原印刷株式会社

ISBN 978-4-7919-7224-1　　　　　　　　　　　　　　　　　　Printed in Japan

7224 聞いて話せる英語演習　Book 2
―頻出表現で学ぶ実用英語―
Listen Up, Talk Back Book 2 —English for Everyday Commun
定価2,530円（本体2,300円＋税10%）

ISBN978-4-7919-7224-1

C1082 ¥2300E

9784791972241

1921082023000

A series designed to brush up communication skills
in situations students will encounter both at home and abroad

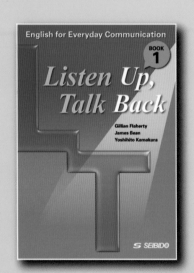

Listen Up, Talk Back Book 1

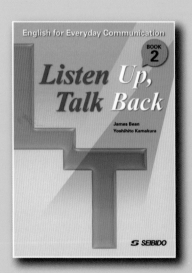

Listen Up, Talk Back Book 2

聖書を生きる

旬人彩人
しゅんじん さいじん

Shunjin Saijin

いのちのことば社